Their World

Their World

Empowering Your Teen to Overcome the Challenges of Adolescence

Laura Chappell

Published by Game Changer Publishing
Cover photo courtesy Johnnyhetfield via iStock

Paperback ISBN: 978-1-962656-23-8
Hardcover ISBN: 978-1-962656-24-5
Digital: ISBN: 978-1-962656-25-2

www.GameChangerPublishing.com

DEDICATION

I dedicate this book to my father. Thank you for
your continuous and unwavering support.
I couldn't have done this without you.
To my mother, my Guardian Angel, words aren't enough.
To my brother, for your encouragement and pride in me.
And to my younger self, my driving force.

Read This First

Just to say thank you for buying and reading my book,
I would love to give you a bundle of free resources!

The bundle includes large colour copies of the figures from this book
and some other useful resources for both you and your teen.

Scan the QR Code Here:

Their World

*Empowering Your Teen to Overcome
the Challenges of Adolescence*

Laura Chappell

www.GameChangerPublishing.com

Preface

This book is for the parents and caregivers of teens in every form they come. You may be a biological, adoptive or foster parent, an official or unofficial step-parent.

You might be an aunt, uncle, or grandparent.

A mentor, coach, or teacher.

A role model.

They may or may not be struggling with the challenges they face, but either way, you want to understand the teen in your life better and help them navigate their adolescent years successfully.

You may even be a teenager wanting to understand and empower yourself.

This book is for anyone who wants the adolescent years to be a positive and rewarding experience for teenagers.

Table of Contents

Introduction

*"Do not predetermine your teen's life for them, but empower
them to forge their own path through the world while
you cheer from the sidelines."*

Teens can change the World.

Whether you agree with me will likely depend on your experience with them,
but I state it as a fact.

The adolescent years are often viewed with trepidation by parents, teens, and
society alike. Teens are collectively seen as challenging, defiant, and
argumentative. They are emotionally volatile, difficult to control and do
stupid, dangerous things. Our once angelic and affectionate children change
overnight into the devil incarnate. They are no longer content and carefree
but emotionally overwhelmed and consumed by what others think.
Adolescence seems to strip away at our children until they become almost
unrecognisable to us, and we stand by confused, frustrated, and helpless, often
adding fuel to the fire in a loving attempt to save them.

There are sobering statistics surrounding adolescents, such as these:

- 1 in 7 (14%) of 10 to 19-year-olds worldwide experience mental
  health disorders (The World Health Organisation, 2022).

- 50% of mental health conditions start by the age of 14.
- (The World Health Organisation, 2022)
- More than 59% of teens in the U.S. (Pew Research Center, 2018) and 44% of teens in Australia (eSafety Commissioner, 2021) have experienced cyberbullying.
- 16 to 19-year-olds are at the highest risk of motor vehicle accidents and three times more likely to be killed in one (CDC, 2020)

But this needn't be the case. Adolescence can be an amazing opportunity for exploration and self-discovery. There are skills and tools your teen can learn so they have a positive experience of adolescence and emerge confidently into adulthood with a well-developed identity and excitement at what life holds.

The very traits that determined their stereotype make teens capable of changing the world. They are risk-takers and thrill-seekers acting despite the consequences; they are defiant and argumentative, resisting and questioning the status quo; they are emotional and intuitive, not yet constrained by reasoning. These traits make successful leaders, innovators, change-makers, activists, advocates, and creatives.

With the right skills and support network, teens are truly capable of achieving greatness. What this looks like depends on the teen and their purpose. They may excel academically, at sport, or with an instrument. They may be a writer, artist, actor, or performer. They may be passionate about human rights, animal welfare, or environmental issues. What's important is they live in alignment with their core values and are allowed to be their authentic self. *Then,* they will absolutely thrive.

Now, I hear you asking, how can you support your teen so they experience adolescence as a positive and enriching one?

Well, that depends, too. I have worked with families, children, and teens for my entire adult life, and I am certain that every parent, child, and parent-child relationship is unique. So, ultimately, what works for one family won't work for another. But, after reading *Their World,* you will understand your teen developmentally, psychologically, physiologically, emotionally, socially, and behaviourally. You will learn how to connect with them at a deeper level, communicate constructively, respond to their needs effectively, and nurture their authentic self. You will have a long list of techniques and approaches at your fingertips to choose from. You will learn to apply the information and tools in this book to your teen as the unique individual *they* are. And you will grow yourself, both as a parent and as the unique individual *you* are.

Their World is the culmination of my life. It taps into 20 years of working in childcare, learning the dynamics of the family unit and how to navigate them successfully. It utilises my training and experience working with young people from a trauma background, including refugee youths, kids in residential and foster care, and victims of child abuse in a specialist child protection unit of the NSW government. It relies on information from my Undergraduate in Psychology, particularly child development, and my Master's in Human Rights, which led me to work in trauma. I include knowledge gained from my current work as a Life and Empowerment Coach for teens and their families and include case studies of my clients to show amazing transformations are possible. Finally, I drew upon my lived experience as a troubled teen who struggled with many of the challenges I address in this book and employ learnings from my lifelong dedication to personal development.

Their World was written because parents like you asked me to after reading articles I posted as part of an online course. They said they loved the easily accessible information, actionable advice, and no-fluff presentation and that the articles were in-depth enough without being overwhelming. They could read each article quickly, get immediate insights, and implement the strategies straight away, getting fast results. As such, *Their World* follows a similar structure to my articles, with the information presented mostly being in list format, with limited bodies of text.

The book has three sections, broken into subsections covering specific topics. It is a collection of small articles you can delve into when you need. It is a parenting reference book and how-to guide.

> *Section 1* contains information on teen development (brain and cognitive development, physical development and puberty, and social development) and its influence on their behaviour. It focuses particularly on a teen's propensity for risky behaviour and how to channel it positively.
>
> *Section 2* discusses all the common challenges teens face during adolescence, such as social media, gaming, bullying, mental illness, vaping, drugs, and alcohol use. Each topic is presented in a similar format, including the facts about it; why a teen is vulnerable to and may engage in it; protective factors; signs to know your teen is struggling with the issue, and what to do about it.
>
> *Section 3* provides Unique Parenting's personal development frameworks and tools for you and your teen to implement, such as The Emotions Wheels, The Building Blocks of Resilience, and Constructive Communication. These strategies can be used to help address any of the issues discussed in the book and give your teen the skills to successfully face the challenges life throws at them. They will also help you develop as a parent and grow as a person.

Their World aims to shift your perspective about your teen and embrace adolescence as the phenomenal experience it can be. Teens are the bridge between childhood and adulthood; they are the ones who materialise change between the generations. Adolescence is the reason you know a different world to your parents and the one to your children. Change comes during adolescence when teens still have the spunk to push against and question the status quo, when society has not yet moulded them into what serves it, and they can chip away at the foundations of what is simply accepted.

This book ultimately empowers your teen to be a changemaker. It does so by helping you understand them by stepping into "their world" and shifting how you experience them. You will see, honour, and accept them for the unique individual they are. *Their World* gives you the tools and strategies to not only support your teen through the challenges of adolescence but to equip them with everything they need to forge their own path through the world and leave it blazing in their wake.

Before we start the book itself, I want to contextualise my position as the author. I believe it is important to acknowledge my privilege as an able-bodied, straight, white, western woman who immigrated to Australia from England in 2011. I am writing through my life lens and do not claim to speak from any other point of view. However, I am not ignorant of the world and have had direct and indirect experiences of different cultures and demographics, of poverty, struggle, grief, and trauma.

My mother was from the Bahamas and grew up in poverty, raised by a single mother after her father died when she was only a young girl, and whom I devastatingly lost to cancer when I was twenty-five. She would share stories of her life, and so I have an understanding and awareness of it through her and its influences on who she became as a woman. My grandmother was from Haiti, and although I have never been, my heritage has always intrigued me. I chose to study Haiti in depth during my Human Rights Masters because of this pull and was shocked by my discoveries. It is the poorest country in the Western hemisphere and has modern-day forms of slavery, including Restaveks, who are domestic child slaves.

I also volunteered in Tanzania when I was 18 years old, teaching English and Geography in a school outside Marangu, a small town at the base of Mount Kilimanjaro. On average, there were 60 students in my class, two or three to a desk and barely younger than me. It was the first time I had any insight into what it felt like to be a minority and actually live in poverty.

I was on the program with another girl, and we lived in teachers' accommodation with a table and a cot each. We were blessed with running water, but it was cold and unsafe to drink, riddled with life-threatening diseases.

There was electricity, but it frequently cut out, robbing us of the ability to boil water for drinking or cooking. It was the only time in my life I felt true hunger or thirst. We washed in buckets of freezing water, and our toilet was a hole in an outhouse. I can't even describe the smell emanating from it as its contents baked in the sweltering heat.

We were paid a teacher's salary to live off. Though this was a good wage for Tanzania, it was nothing compared to the money I was used to having. My months there were life-changing and largely contributed to the person I am today. Why? It was the realisation that even living in such poverty, the teens I worked with and the people I met were happier, more grateful, more generous, and more caring than the fortunate and privileged people I knew from home—including myself.

My work in child protection and as a mentor to a girl from a disadvantaged background exposed me to situations of poverty, abuse, and neglect here in Australia, where over 3 million people live below the poverty line, including more than 760,000 children. I saw first-hand generational trauma and dysfunctional cycles being repeated. I witnessed desperate parents trying their best with the limited knowledge and tools they had to manage their teens' behaviour. I worked with teens from "good" backgrounds who were lost, struggling, and distressed, who lashed out at their parents and the world around them, and who hurt themselves in the process.

There are topics and demographics of people I have limited experience with and am not an expert in, for example, differently abled and neuro-diverse teens. I will not go into detail about different faiths or religious beliefs, cultural backgrounds, sexualities, or gender identities either. But you can apply the majority of what I recommend to any teen as my approach focuses on the individual and their need to be seen, heard, understood, and accepted for who they are. So, even if your teen falls into the categories I have mentioned, this book is still for you.

SECTION 1

THEIR BEHAVIOUR IS THE SYMPTOM

CHAPTER 1

The Nuts and Bolts of Teen Development

"The adolescent years are the most developmentally challenging of your child's life at a time they are ill equipped to handle them. Be a little easier on them."

Being aware of your teens' development will shed new light on their behaviour and you will understand the "whys" behind what they do. Your teen's behaviour is a symptom of intricately intertwined factors driven by the psychological, emotional, physiological, and innate social needs ignited by the onset of adolescence.

The adolescent years are the most rapid period of development in your teen's life and is the transitional phase between childhood and adulthood. It is when they reach cognitive, emotional, physical, social, and sexual maturation (referred to as puberty). It can be a confronting, confusing, and frightening time for your teenager as they face massive changes while largely lacking the ability to cope with them.

Although adolescence starts around 10 years of age and finishes at about 19, the rate of development can vary greatly between boys and girls and between individuals, which can mould how they experience life in ways that may or may not be obvious. So, knowing what's happening developmentally with your teen in relation to their peers will also help you understand them better, pre-empt possible challenges, and mitigate them.

Teens are often unaware of what is happening to them during adolescence, and they struggle to identify and communicate their thoughts, feelings, and needs, which are reflected in and expressed through their behaviour. So, by helping them understand the basics of what's going on for them developmentally, and with the right tools and support, you can assist your teen to experience adolescence as an exciting, rewarding, and fulfilling time.

Brain and Cognitive Development

Brain development refers to changes in the physical structure of your teen's brain, while cognitive development refers to the way your teen uses their brain. Your teenager's brain will have reached its full size physically by the age of eleven in girls and around fourteen in boys. However, their brains do not completely mature until their mid to late 20s.

Synaptic pruning is a process that occurs in your teenager's brain during adolescence. Synapses are the connections between brain cells that allow messages in the form of chemical and electrical signals to pass between the neurons (nerve cells). The purpose of this pruning process is to make their brain more efficient, which is done by strengthening the pathways your teen frequently used during childhood (because they are identified as important) while disposing of extra neurons and synapses. For example, your primary language at home is English, so your teen's brain hardwires the pathways associated with understanding, speaking and writing English. However, if they learned French when they were ten but no longer took classes or practised the language, these connections would be pruned away.

The pruning process starts at the back of the brain and finishes with the prefrontal cortex at the front. The issue with this is the prefrontal cortex plays a really important role in higher-level cognitive functioning, including judgement, decision-making, planning, and impulse control. Therefore, being the last area to mature means your teenager's ability to make decisions, plan and think about consequences, problem solve, and control their impulses are all impeded. Furthermore, this means your teen relies on an area of the brain called the amygdala much more than adults do. The amygdala is responsible for emotions, impulses, aggression, and instinctive behaviours, which is why your teen may appear erratic, reactive, and confrontational.

Add to this, your teen's brain is more sensitive to a hormone called dopamine, also known as the "happy hormone." Dopamine is involved in the brain's reward system and is responsible for motivation, drive, and focus. The result is your teen is more likely to seek out pleasurable experiences, regardless of the risk. This is why teens are known for their propensity for risk-taking, and it is something we will explore in the next chapter.

Figure 1.

A Quick Guide to
Teenage Brain Development

The brain reaches its full size at around 11yrs for girls and 14yrs for boys (think both fists next to each other). However it does not attain maturity until mid to late twenties meaning teens are navigating the challenges of life without a completely developed brain (approx 80%)

Dopamine is known as the 'happy hormone' and is involved in the brains reward system as it motivates, drives and focuses the brain. Adolescent brains are more sensitive to dopamine, as such, they have a higher inclination to seek pleasure, despite potential risk

A process of pruning occurs in adolescence to make the brain more efficient. Connections built during childhood that are commonly used are now strengthened and those left unused are lost

With lack of development in the prefrontal cortex, teenagers rely more on the amygdala than adults to make decisions and problem solve. The amygdala is associated with emotions, impulse, aggression, and instinctive behaviour. As a reult teenagers can seem erratic, reactive and confrontational

The prefrontal cortex is the last part of the brain to 'connect'. It is responsible for judgement, decision making, planning & impulse control. As such, teenagers ability to make decisions, plan/think about consequences, problem solve and control impulses are impacted

Physical Development and Puberty

Puberty is the period during which your teen's body matures from a child's into an adult's and becomes capable of reproduction. Puberty starts at around 8 to 13 years old in girls and 9 to 14 in boys and lasts approximately 2 to 5 years. During puberty, your teen experiences many physical changes in various stages.

Professor Tanner was a child development expert who identified the visible stages of puberty and developed a guideline to describe the changes that children and teens experience during this time. It is called the Tanner Stages or sexual maturity rating (SMR). Tanner Stages of Puberty for females are set out in Figure 2 and for males in Figure 3 at the end of this section. Share these with your teen so they are aware of the physical changes they can expect during puberty and understand where they are developmentally.

The stages Tanner developed have an age range, so it is completely normal for a teen to experience these physical changes at varying times, depending on the individual. However, if your teen experiences puberty outside of these "normal" ranges, several factors could be responsible. The following have been found to, directly and indirectly, influence the onset of puberty:

1) Genetics: a family history of delayed or disturbed puberty usually predicts a teen will also experience a delay or disruption to theirs. Those with a family history of early-onset puberty will also likely start puberty earlier.
2) Low birth weight has been linked to the early onset of puberty and menarche (first period) in girls but later development in boys.
3) Overweight or obese children usually start puberty earlier than those in the "normal" weight range and may experience prolonged puberty.
4) Underweight children may start puberty later than peers in the "normal" weight range.

5) Poor nutrition delays puberty due to malnutrition.

6) Malnutrition from disorders such as anorexia or bulimia; diseases with malabsorption, such as inflammatory bowel disease; or diseases that have systemic impacts like cystic fibrosis, all delay puberty.

7) Environmental chemicals such as bisphenol A (BPA), which occur in plastics, have been associated with the early onset of puberty and/or its rapid progression.

8) Stress might trigger puberty early.

9) Children who have experienced violence may start puberty early.

10) Poverty has been associated with early onset of puberty.

During puberty, your teen will not only experience physical changes but also emotional ones. Their emotions will fluctuate and be more intense due to changes in the hormones testosterone, oestrogen, and progesterone. Their emotions will likely be erratic and difficult to manage. This can be particularly true for girls around their menstrual cycle, so I would highly recommend your teen track their cycle and note any physical symptoms, feelings, and thoughts related to it so they can start to identify patterns (A Menstrual Cycle Diary is included in the Free Resources Bundle).

For example, they may feel especially sensitive and get short-tempered or easily upset during their period. They may have a lot less energy the week before they bleed and need more rest instead of them "just being lazy." It is a great habit to get into earlier on so she becomes aware of her body and its needs as a woman. Even exercise can be optimally designed around her cycle. Tracking her cycle will also help you understand and preempt her behaviour. You will be better able to support her and establish a routine that sinks with her cycle.

For instance, your daughter is responsible for fewer chores when she lacks energy and motivation just before and during her bleed, but does a few extra chores when she is ovulating and feels like superwoman!

The age your teenager starts puberty and the rate at which they develop can have a huge impact on their experience of adolescence. Understanding where your teen is developmentally compared to their peers can help predict and mitigate any challenges they may face. For example, if your teenage girl develops breasts earlier than her peers, she may become self-conscious about her body. She may also be teased because of the size of her breasts and feel isolated because she is different from her peers. As a sense of belonging is fundamental to a teen's development, being teased can impact her confidence, self-esteem, and mental health. She may also be sexualised by boys earlier than she's ready to explore her sexuality.

If your teen is a boy and behind their friends developmentally, they may be shorter than their peers and be unable to grow facial hair. This can impact their self-esteem as they may feel extremely self-conscious and childlike compared to their maturing friends. You can see from these examples the ripple effect your teen's physical development has on their social experiences and how, in turn, that can impact their mental health.

Figure 2.

Tanner Stages of Puberty : Females

TANNER STAGE	AGE STARTS (Typically)	NOTICEABLE PHYSICAL CHANGES
STAGE 1	After their 8th birthday	None (The brain releases hormones preparing the body for changes)
STAGE 2	From 9 to 11 years old	Breast 'buds' start to form and areola expand; uterus begins to get larger; small amounts of pubic hair grows on lips of vulva
STAGE 3	After 12 years of age	Breast 'buds' continue to grow; pubic hair thickens; underarm hair starts to grow; acne may start appearing on face & back; greatest height growth rate occurs (approx 3.2 inches per yr); hips & thighs start fattening
STAGE 4	Around 13 years old	Breasts become fuller; many start menstruation (typically 12-14 but can be earlier); height growth slows; pubic hair thickens
STAGE 5	Around 15 years old	Breasts reach approximate adult size (though can continue to grow until 18); periods regulate after 6 months - 2yrs; pubic hair grows to thighs; genitals & reproductive organs completely developed; hips, thighs & buttocks fill out
		Puberty ends between 14 and 16 for most girls

Figure 3.

Tanner Stages of Puberty : Males

TANNER STAGE	AGE STARTS (Typically)	NOTICEABLE PHYSICAL CHANGES
STAGE 1	After their 9th or 10th birthday	None (The brain releases hormones preparing the body for changes)
STAGE 2	Around 11 years old	Testicles & surrounding skin (scrotum) begin to grow; pubic hair starts to form on the penis base
STAGE 3	Around 13 years old	Penis starts lengthening & testes continue to grow larger; begin having wet dreams (nighttime ejaculation); voice begins to occilate between high & low pitch; some breast tissue may form under nipples but goes away within a couple of years; muscle growth; height growth (2-32. inch per yr)
STAGE 4	Around 14 years old	Penis, testes & scrotum continue growing & scrotum darkens in colour; armpit hair starts to grow; voice becomes permanently deep; acne may appear
STAGE 5	Around 15 years old	Penis, testicles & scrotum are fully grown; pubic hair fills out & spread to thighs; facial hair starts to grow; height growth slows; muscles continue to develop
		Puberty completed for most boys by age 18

Social Development

Socially, the adolescent years are also fundamental to your teen's identity formation.

It is completely normal for your teen to start pulling away from you and spend increasingly larger amounts of time socialising and bonding with their peers. At first, they will have a small, close-knit group of same-sex friends who provide a sense of belonging. As they grow older, they will form friendships with the opposite sex, start to have romantic relationships, and explore couplehood. So when your teen distances themself from you, they're responding to an innate biological drive to separate from their parents. They will also start to sever emotional bonds with you in preparation for exploring the emotional intimacy of couplehood.

During this time, conflict between you and your teen will likely escalate in intensity and frequency due to them seeking independence and pushing boundaries. Identity development theorists such as Erickson and Marcia believe teens experience an identity crisis during which they try to discover a sense of self and answer the existential question, *Who Am I?* During this period, your teen will grapple to resolve the conflict between their personal and socially satisfactory desires. This process drives them toward growth and differentiation as they explore options, make choices, and settle on an outcome. These decisions will be in relation to everything, including their appearance, sexuality, educational vocation and career aspirations, personal, political, and social views, interests, and even their personality. This may look indecisive from the outside. For example, they want pink hair one moment and black the next, or they were obsessed with soccer last month, and now it's surfing. But it's all part of the journey of self-discovery.

If your teen is successful at forming a well-developed identity, they will have settled on values, beliefs, and goals they are aligned with and committed to as an adolescent and will adhere to into an adult. These values, beliefs, and goals may or may not align with yours, but with their peer group, and though it may be difficult to accept, that's okay. In fact, some of your teen's values and beliefs will probably align with their peers, as peer bonds are increasingly more important during these years. Talk to them about it and be curious about why they have chosen their values and beliefs. It will help you understand your teen better and form a deeper connection with them, something that's extremely important to their well-being (despite their pulling away). If you condemn their choices, they will likely be deceptive about their decisions and actions.

If your teen does not form a well-developed identity, they will not have a strong sense of who they are or their role in the world. This can impact their confidence and self-esteem, make them more vulnerable to peer pressure, lack commitment and fortitude in relationships and activities, and be self-orientated and self-indulgent. On the subject of peer pressure, teens are already susceptible to peer pressure because of their need to belong and fit in with the social network. This is why it's so important to not only allow but encourage your teen to ask questions, try new experiences, and explore the world so they can form a strong identity and discover who they are as an individual, not just as your child and under your guiding principles.

Try not to be offended if they don't want to be seen in public with you or find you embarrassing, as it is a normal part of social maturation. It also means they are confident in your relationship and feel comfortable to momentarily take it for granted. They will also likely be inconsistent, wanting nothing to do with you one day and then desiring all your focus the next. During the adolescent years, they have one foot in childhood and the other in adulthood, skipping between the two worlds to explore who they are. It can be exciting, frightening, fun, and challenging. As their parents, it can be difficult, but try to give them the freedom to explore their identity while providing them the support and guidance they need.

Conclusion

Your teen will experience the most rapid period of growth during their adolescent years as their psychological, emotional, physical, and social worlds are upheaved. It can be a terrifying and uncomfortable time for your teen, as their body changes in embarrassing ways; they have uncontrollable mood swings and emotions they don't know how to manage; they may feel lost as they question who they are, confused at wanting the safety of home while having the urge to pull away under the internal drive to seek belonging among their peers. But this needn't be the case. If your teen knows what to expect during adolescence and is prepared for it, they can have an adventurous time!

CHAPTER 2

Adolescence, It's a Risky Business!

"Risky behaviour can be empowering or problematic. With the right tools, your teen could change the world. Without them, they could burn it to the ground."

What is normal risk-taking behaviour? And why do teens engage in it? As we covered under teenage development in chapter one, because your teen's brain is not yet fully developed, they are more inclined to engage in risky behaviour and seek out experiences that make them feel good, regardless of the potential negative consequences.

"Unique Parenting" defines normal teenage risk-taking as any behaviour or decision a teen makes, consciously or unconsciously, where they perceive the outcome to be uncertain or of more value to them in the short term versus any long-term benefit.

Although risk-taking often has negative connotations when associated with teenage behaviour, if channelled properly, it is also a positive and important part of them forming a well-developed identity.

Normal Risk-Taking Behaviour

What is normal and positive risk-taking behaviour?

1) *Testing their abilities.*

They are pushing themselves in areas such as sport, music, and language and taking on new challenges where their abilities are being stretched. They are competing in activities and taking on responsibilities such as leadership roles at school.

2) *Claiming independence.*

They are pulling away from you and forming closer relationships with their friends. They are making decisions based on their individual needs rather than your expectations.

3) *Seeking new experiences.*

They are doing things outside of the norm, such as trying new activities, going to different places, and starting new hobbies.

4) *Exploring limits.*

This can show up as your teen being defiant or argumentative, but they're exploring limitations imposed on them and finding ways to negotiate new ones.

5) *Finding their identity.*

Your teen will seek their identity and separate from their role as your child through their friendships and experiences. They may seem to stop and start different activities, alter their appearance, and constantly change their mind about things, but this is all normal and part of self-exploration.

If their propensity for risky behaviour is channelled positively, your teen will have the capacity to forge a path for themselves and drive change in "their world." The ability to take risks can make them innovators and change makers as they aren't being kept small by fear. They can be activists and advocates because they are not scared to stand up for those without a voice or for causes that mean something to them. They can be leaders, inspiring others to take risks, think outside the box, and act contradictory to what society says is possible. Your teen can accomplish phenomenal things with the right support, tools, and encouragement.

These are just three young people who have already impacted the world of activism and are a true inspiration.

Miley Dyas

Miley was 11 years old when she noticed most children's books lacked cultural diversity and had few female protagonists. In response, she started the #1000 Black Girl Books Drive to collect 1,000 books with black female protagonists so girls like her could see themselves represented in literature. Since then, Miley has spoken at the White House and at the United Nations. She has written her own book, was named one of the most influential teens by Time in 2018, and is the youngest member of Forbes 30 under 30 to date.

Jaylen Arnold

Jaylen was bullied because of his differences. He was diagnosed as a child with Tourette's syndrome, obsessive-compulsive disorder, and Asperger's syndrome. Due to his experiences, Jaylen started the Jaylens Challenge Foundation to educate children on bullying prevention with the purpose of ending childhood bullying. Jalyn had this concept when he was only eight years old. In 2014, he was nominated as a World of Children Honorary and received the Princess Diana Legacy Award for Philanthropy in 2019.

Jazz Jennings

Jazz is an LGBT rights activist and speaks openly about her experiences as a transgender woman. Jazz was only six years old when she went on national TV and said that despite what her birth certificate said, she was a girl. She founded the Purple Rainbow Foundation to increase awareness and enhance the lives of transgender children and teenagers. At the time of writing, her foundation had raised over $100,000 to support transgender youth. Jazz has contributed largely to the recognition of transgender people in U.S. mainstream media shows by speaking out and is the co-author of two children's books based on her experiences.

Activity: Suggest your teen research young people who have made an impact in areas they are interested in to show them what is possible and inspire them to take action.

Problematic Risk-Taking Behaviour

When does risk-taking behaviour become problematic, and what can you do about it? Teens can lose their way for a number of reasons and start engaging in risky behaviours that are detrimental to their well-being.

"Unique Parenting" defines problematic risk-taking behaviour as normal developmental risk-taking that has escalated to the degree it negatively impacts the teen in any or all areas of their life. This could be at school, home, or in the wider community and affects them emotionally, physically, psychologically, socially, and/or academically. Their behaviours have become concerning to the people who care for them, and they have little evidence of calming down. Interventions may or may not have been tried but with limited to no success.

Your teen's need for connection and belonging can make them vulnerable to peer pressure. They will want to adapt and conform to the group norms, which may include engaging in less than desirable activities, such as substance use, stealing, skipping school, and taking liberties with their own and others' physical safety. There is evidence boys are more likely to engage in risky behaviour and take drugs, while girls are more likely to develop internalised disorders such as anxiety and depression. However, girls may engage in risky behaviour and or substance use as a coping mechanism or numbing strategy due to their mental health illnesses.

These are examples of behaviours where risk-taking and thrill-seeking is problematic and concerning. If your teenager is doing any of these, they should be addressed:

1) They are socialising with peers who encourage more extreme risk-taking behaviour.
2) They are putting themselves and/or others at risk of physical harm; e.g., doing dares such as jumping off high walls or racing cars.
3) They are engaging in promiscuous behaviour and/or unsafe sexual activity.
4) They have a disregard for authority, be it you, their teachers, or officials such as the police, rather than just questioning it.
5) They are increasingly engaged in antisocial behaviour and/or breaking the law. For example, they start with shoplifting some food, and it escalates to stealing a peer's bicycle from school.
6) They are regularly taking substances such as drugs and alcohol rather than experimenting with or trying them. They're taking dangerous substances for recreational purposes, such as chroming, where they inhale volatile substances to get high (chroming is an activity named after the chrome-based paint trend that it initially started with).

On this note, I'd recommend getting educated on any TikTok trends that encourage dangerous behaviours, such as chroming. Teens are particularly susceptible to being swept up in the hype and trying these trends. For example, the Cha Cha Slide Challenge in 2022, where drivers would listen to the song Mr. C, the Slide Man, and drive according to the lyrics "slide left" when they would drive into oncoming traffic.

Or the Benadryl Challenge, where users ingest a large amount of Benadryl to trigger hallucinations, which can be fatal. Ask your teens if they are aware of these trends and discuss the dangers with them. Make a plan of action if they feel pressured into taking part in one of these trends. Helping your teen to strengthen their sense of self and form a well-established identity will make them less susceptible to peer pressure. Knowing who they are will help them disengage from these destructive activities, have the confidence to say no to doing things they don't want to, and even end friendships in favour of finding ones that align with their values and beliefs.

There are healthy ways your teen can channel their propensity for risk-taking, and I would recommend you encourage them to engage in any of the following if you have concerns about their current behaviour.

1) *Enter a competition.*

   It could be sports, music or debating, a team or solo activity. Anything your teen enjoys! The body produces adrenaline in preparation for competing, similar to when your teen engages in a risk-taking activity so they will get the same "rush" but in a positive way. Also, the process of getting competition ready channels their emotions, assists with impulse control, and improves decision-making.

2) *Perform.*

   Performing has the same effect as entering a competition. Your teen could be in a play or show, join a band or orchestra. Anything that entails standing in front of an audience and puts them outside of their comfort zone, invoking feelings of "danger."

3) *Release aggression in healthy ways.*

   Attempting to suppress aggressive feelings may lead to explosive outbursts. Have your teen focus their aggression in a safe, controlled environment so they can release it. Boxing and martial arts are great, as they also require discipline. Other contact sports assist with releasing aggression and rely on teamwork. Running and swimming have also been shown to relieve aggression. They could use stress toys or punch pillows if your teen is not keen on sport.

4. *Learn something new.*
   This pushes them outside of their comfort zone, which will cause the body to perceive it is in danger and respond accordingly, giving them a rush of adrenaline as the body prepares for fight-or-flight. This could be learning an instrument, a sport, a new language, or any other skill.

5) *Do something challenging.*
   Your teen could do something they find challenging, such as holding a snake at the local zoo if they're scared of snakes or going in a hot air balloon if they don't like heights. This gives them a sense of risk-taking and of achievement once they've done it.

6) *Do something scary.*
   They could try adrenaline sports like hang gliding, rock climbing, or track racing. It's risk-taking done in a much safer and controlled environment. Obviously, this needs to be age-appropriate.

7) *Play and have fun.*
   Your teen could go to a theme park, try go-karting, head to an arcade, play laser tag or paintball, anything that gets that blood pumping in a fun way. And as a bonus, laughter increases the happy hormones dopamine, serotonin, and oxytocin and releases endorphins, the feel-good hormones, so they'll both be channelling their propensity for risk-taking and boosting their mood.

Engaging in these activities will also expose your teen to different types of people and facilitate meeting new friends with whom they can form genuine connections over shared interests. This may divert them from the problematic risk-taking behaviour they were engaging in with their old friends.

At-Risk

There is a final group of adolescents we need to discuss. Some teenagers are deemed "at-risk," meaning they are in danger of being physically, psychologically, or emotionally harmed or dying, either because of their own actions or circumstances outside of their control (as defined by Unique Parenting).

The following may result in the teen being "at-risk."

1) They are facing mental health challenges such as anxiety, depression, or eating disorders.
2) They are exhibiting self-harming behaviours, including cutting or burning, or putting themselves in situations they may be physically harmed.
3) They have disengaged from family, school, and their community despite having a support network that cares for them.
4) They are socially isolated, with few or no friends, and have limited family support.
5) They are experiencing or have experienced neglect, trauma, abuse, or family and domestic violence.
6) They live in extreme poverty and do not have their basic needs met.

I will not discuss this in any more depth because it is an entire book on its own. However, it is important you know how to identify at-risk teens because it is fundamental they have extra support and will require some form of professional intervention. If you believe your teen falls into any of these categories, please get professional assistance immediately. And if any teen you know raises concerns, report them to the school, police, child protection helpline, or another appropriate authority figure. You can do this anonymously if you have any fear of repercussions.

Conclusion

Risky behaviour is a normal and healthy part of adolescence. When channelled correctly, it drives them to explore the world and develop a well-defined identity. However, some teens get lost and engage in risky behaviours that become problematic and negatively impact their well-being. I will discuss these behaviours in depth in Section 2. As a parent, being aware of the signs means you can support your teen to redirect and channel their propensity for risk-taking in constructive ways.

Figure 4.

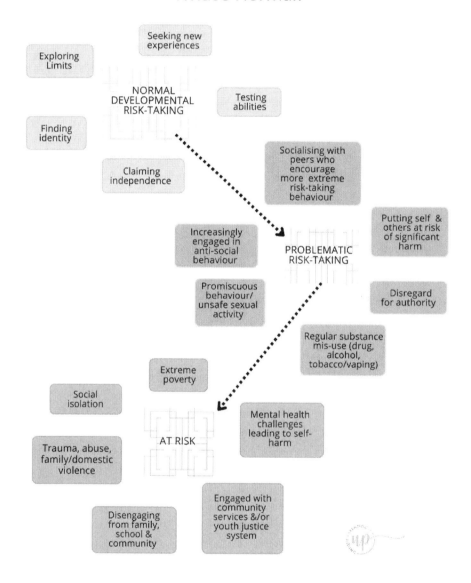

Teenage Risk-Taking Behaviour: What's Normal?

SECTION 2

THE ISSUES WITH ADOLESCENCE

CHAPTER 3

Relationships in All their Forms

"Don't underestimate the importance of supportive relationships.
A sense of belonging is fundamental to your teen's well-being
and their success in life."

Relationships in all their weird and wonderful forms are an important and integral part of your teen's development. By strengthening your connection with your teen and empowering them with the knowledge and skills to explore their identity, they will become strong, confident, and self-assured individuals. They will contribute to family life, have the ability to form positive friendships, engage in healthy sexual and romantic relationships, and successfully navigate the challenges that come with these social connections when they arise.

Although I will discuss different types of relationships separately, such as family, friendships and peers, and romantic relationships, many of the challenges are intertwined, and the tools needed to improve these relationships are the same, just applied differently.

The Family

Families come in all shapes and sizes. There are nuclear families and extended families; adoptive, fostered, and blended families; two-household families and single-parent families; families with same-sex parents; and multiple parents. There are chosen families. Each one comes with their own blessings and challenges when it comes to their children entering the teenage years. But most of the challenges have common threads running through them, so the tools I will discuss can be used in all of them by applying your family's lens to them.

You will likely have noticed an increase in the intensity and frequency of conflict between you and your teen and your teen with others. As we discussed in Chapter One, this is normal during adolescence. However, conflict may be exacerbated if you do not allow your teen to explore their identity through friendships and other experiences. By enforcing strict rules, they are more likely to rebel and push against them. These rules will also encourage your teen to be deceptive, as they will still have the drive to find themselves and so do it behind your back.

Activity: Instead of setting house rules, collaborate on them with your teen. They may surprise you. Firstly, I recommend referring to them as boundaries rather than rules, as this word immediately sets up a dictatorial dynamic from your teen's perspective.

1. Have a family meeting for the specific purpose of discussing boundaries at a time when everyone can be fully present. Each person brings ideas about what they believe are fair boundaries. These could be around bedtime and curfew, social media, gaming and mobile phone use, family time, household responsibilities, and general expectations. Address two or three at a time so it doesn't become overwhelming.

   Note: these boundaries are not just for your teen but include all family members. Make sure everyone has enough time to properly prepare.

2. Each family member has an equal opportunity to express their ideas and explain the reasoning behind them. For example, you say bedtime is at 9:30; otherwise, your teen is too tired to be productive at school.

3. After everyone has spoken, discuss and set them. If you find it difficult to decide on a boundary, compromise, or even toss a coin. For example, one boundary could be bedtime at 9:30 p.m. during the school week and term time, while on Friday and Saturday evenings and during school holidays, it is 10:30 p.m.

4. In the same way, establish consequences for breaking the boundaries. They must be relative, fair, and proportionate. For example, if your teen doesn't go to bed at the appropriate time and they are tired, they will need to go to bed earlier for two nights to catch up on the sleep they missed.

5. Re-visit these boundaries every three months in case one isn't working or to set a new boundary. By having your teen collaborate on setting household boundaries, they are more likely to both abide by them and accept any consequences of breaking them. This process also teaches them skills such as effective communication and problem solving and how to negotiate and compromise; it gives them a level of autonomy over decisions that impact them and shows you value and respect their opinions. It also helps them think about long-term consequences, something teens struggle with due to their brain development.

As adolescence can be destabilising for teenagers, it is important their family and home life are as secure and consistent as possible. Despite what they might think, teens need boundaries to feel safe and loved, especially when every aspect of their life feels out of control. Boundaries ground them. Once these boundaries are in place, you can have the confidence to allow your teen greater independence and autonomy over their lives. I understand it can be hard at times as your teen may seem to be the cause of all the drama, and I acknowledge it can be challenging to give them the freedom to explore their identity and enforce boundaries while remaining connected to them, but it is possible.

1) *Remind yourself that conflict and your teen's desire to pull away from you is a normal and healthy stage of development.* In fact, it means they are secure in their relationship with you and feel safe to momentarily take it for granted. Understanding this fact can bring you comfort, stop you from taking their actions personally, and prevent you from pushing them away even further through your often unconscious behaviour. You may even choose to celebrate this important life stage as many cultures do, rather than fear it or mourn what it was.

2) *Help them understand what's going on during this developmental stage.* Helping your teen understand what's going on for them, or finding someone who can, can ease this transition for them and enable them to both identify and verbalise what's going on for them in the light of their developmental stage. This, in turn, helps maintain your connection because they will be less likely to lash out or withdraw when they feel confused or overwhelmed.

3) *Equip your teens with the tools they need to thrive in the world.* Teach them both soft skills such as constructive communication, setting healthy boundaries, identifying and expressing their needs, and life

skills such as cooking, nutrition, and financial literacy. The more you prepare your teen for independence, the more comfortable you will be with letting them go. They will be more confident in themselves, their abilities, and decision-making and more likely to turn to you when they need help. It is often teens who lack confidence and self-esteem who make bad judgement calls and hide things from their parents, causing further distance in the relationship.

4) *Keep avenues of communication open.* Let your teen know you're available to talk whenever they need about anything they want, and most importantly, without judgement. This doesn't mean without consequences. If they know you provide a safe space for them, they will turn towards you when things get challenging instead of away from you. And as we all know, communication is key to a successful relationship.

5) *Find an activity just for the two of you.* Find an activity to do with your teen that gives you quality time together and the opportunity to connect. Something new is even better as you'll both be novices and can learn together, and this helps reduce the power imbalance between "parent" and "teen." You will start to see your teen as an individual person and interact with them differently by learning something new. Your teen will see you are someone who doesn't know everything, is fallible and is willing to be vulnerable. This will both strengthen your connection and make it easier for them to approach you with problems.

6) *Do something as a family.* Do an activity that requires you to collaborate, or simply something you enjoy. All members of the family need to agree on the activity, and as this is a time for connection, it cannot be competitive as this risks conflict.

7) *Focus on yourself.* It can be especially difficult when your teen pulls away because your role and identity as a parent can feel in jeopardy. You will always be a parent, but the way this looks will continue to change. Just as your responsibilities were different when they were a baby, a toddler, eight or twelve, they will continue to develop during their teenage years. Use this opportunity to explore who you are in this new stage of parenting. Find new hobbies, socialise with your friends, increase self-care, and go on date nights. Focusing on yourself can also reduce the feeling of abandonment you have in response to your teen's increasing need for independence, and it will be easier to let them go. I assure you, your teen will sense this, and your relationship will benefit from it. Furthermore, you will be role-modelling what independence and identity are to your teen precisely at the time they need them. Remember, they are more effectively influenced by what you do than what you say.

Case Study: Millie, 13 years old
(name changed for confidentiality)

The Struggle

Millie was extremely challenging for her parents, and her behaviour was escalating. She was staying out of the house for long periods of time and skipped school regularly. Her parents were often unaware of where she was. Millie spent most nights at her boyfriend's house without their approval, and she was threatening to move in with him. She was stealing cash from her parents, and they removed the door from her bedroom due to their mistrust of her, which further exacerbated the situation. Both Millie's parents worked long hours and were tired when they got home, so they rarely did anything as a family, and Millie often took care of herself.

The Transformation

I worked with both Millie and her parents. With Millie, we started by helping her identify her feelings using the emotions wheels. We discovered under all her anger, which she aimed at her parents, were feelings of resentment, having to care for herself, and sadness because she felt lonely, abandoned, and unimportant to her parents. She stayed with her boyfriend a lot because she felt a sense of belonging being in a household where his family was close. Millie also felt unsafe with the door off as she felt exposed and didn't have a space completely of her own. The lack of a door meant anyone could come in whenever they wanted. Her bedroom door symbolised boundaries for her and they were completely crossed without her consent.

I worked on constructive communication with both Millie and her parents so Millie could tell them how she really felt about life at home, and her parents would listen without becoming defensive. They were actually saddened and surprised by Millie's revelations. Millie's parents were also able to communicate the impact Millie's behaviour was having on them. They sat down as a family and collaborated on household boundaries, to which all agreed, eventually.

They also scheduled a family night every week and special family activities once a month. Millie's door was put back on, and her parents needed to ask her consent before entering. Millie also, in turn, was to respect their property and stopped stealing. Millie felt loved and valued by her parents, and they spent more time together as a family, even if it was just watching TV or eating together. Millie's boyfriend spent time at her house rather than Millie always going to his, and he got to know her parents. They respected Millie's parents' wishes about him not sleeping over at her age, and they trusted her to have him in the room with her door shut. There was a lot less conflict between Millie and her parents as they were able to communicate constructively, and where arguments did arise, they managed to resolve it quickly.

Friends and Peer Relationships

Friendships and peer relationships will become increasingly more important to your teen as they grow older. These connections are fundamental to your teen's development as they explore their identity and find their role in the world. Positive relationships will help your teen evolve a well-developed identity with strong values, beliefs, and worthwhile goals. They will have higher levels of self-esteem and self-worth. They will have stronger boundaries, be less inclined to engage in problematic risk-taking behaviours or substance misuse, and have lower rates of mental health challenges. They will also be more successful.

So, how do you help your teen form and maintain positive, healthy relationships?

1) Help them identify their values. Knowing their values means they can form friendships with teens who have shared values, giving them a stronger connection than friendships based on less solid foundations, such as being neighbours, or your friends' kids. They can also use values such as kindness and honesty, to guide their treatment of others and to decide whether they want to maintain friendships that may no longer align with their values (an extensive Values List is included in the Free Resources Bundle).

2) Suggest they have hobbies and engage in extracurricular activities so they meet other teens with common interests.

3) Encourage them to spend quality time with their friends and facilitate it. This may look like driving them to meet their friends, having them over to your house, or paying for them to do an activity.

4) Teach your teens to have healthy boundaries and learn to say no to things they don't want to do. This will help prevent arguments, feelings of resentment, or talking behind each other's backs.

5) Help them understand the importance of supporting, caring friendships so they learn to value the ones they have and treat them well.

6) Assist them in building resilience so they bounce back from disagreements and disappointments in their friendships (see Chapter 7).

7) Learning constructive communication will help your teen communicate their opinions and needs in an assertive and healthy manner (see Chapter 8).

8) Building emotional intelligence means your teen will be able to identify and express their emotions, be aware of their friend's emotions, and hold space for them (see Chapter 6).

9) Help them improve their self-awareness so they can honestly reflect on their thoughts, feelings, and behaviours, and how they may be contributing to a situation, such as an argument with their friend (see Chapter 9).

10) Role model positive friendships so your teen can see what a good friend looks like in practice.

No matter how positive your teen's friendship group is, they will have arguments. It can be extremely difficult for your teen to navigate conflict and deal with the breakdown of friendships, especially because a sense of belonging is so important to their identity.

So, how can you support your teen through these tough times when they arise?

1) *Listen.* Let your teen speak freely about what's going on for them without interruption or trying to find solutions.

2) *Acknowledge their situation.* It may seem insignificant to you, but the issue may be huge for your teen. Validate their feelings and be empathetic about how hard it must be for them.

3) *Do not speak negatively or judge their friend's actions towards your teen.* Your teen needs you to role model appropriate behaviour and criticising their friend is not healthy or constructive. If you need to vent because you're upset for your teen, do so when they are not around and to a trusted adult. Also, they're very likely to be friends again when things have settled, so you need to process your own feelings about the situation before that happens.

4) *Help your teen identify their feelings.* They might think they are angry, but in fact, they feel sad their friend betrayed them. Then, assist them to process their feelings and understand where these feelings might be coming from (see Chapter 6).

5) *Discuss the possibility their friend may have a different experience of what happened.* Brainstorm with your teen some reasons their friend might have done or said what they did, no matter how silly. This will assist your teen to understand their perspective is not the only one. This process will also teach them empathy and increase their emotional intelligence (see Chapter 6).

6) *Help your teen problem-solve.* Find different ways they could address the situation or solve the problem, and choose the best option. You could even role-play what they might say to build their confidence.

7) *Help your teen with their communication skills* so they can address the issue with their friend in a constructive manner and hopefully resolve it (see conflict and communication in Chapter 8).

8) *Friendships can be for a reason, a season, or a lifetime.* Have your teen reflect on the friendship and decide if it is still something they want in their lives or whether they have outgrown the friendship, in which case they could form new ones based on who they are now.

Friendships and relationships that are toxic or unhealthy can have an extremely negative impact on your teen socially, emotionally, psychologically, and physiologically. They are more likely to engage in risky behaviour due to peer pressure and group norms. They are less likely to participate in school, set achievable career and vocational goals, or be involved in social groups or their community. They will have weaker boundaries, lower levels of self-esteem, and be more vulnerable to mental health challenges. Furthermore, they are more inclined to be bullies, support bullying behaviour, and be the target of bullying themselves.

Bullying

The United Nations Educational, Scientific, and Cultural Organization, UNESCO, found almost one in three teens are being bullied worldwide. This is a frightening statistic given the strong and lasting effects bullying has on a teen's mental and emotional health throughout adolescence.

Bullying is abuse. It is the deliberate harm, intimidation, or coercion of someone perceived as vulnerable. It entails repeated threats, insults, or jesting over a period of time and can have long-term, dire impacts on the person being targeted. It can cause emotional, physical, social and/or psychological harm.

Bullying can take different forms.

1) Verbally and done straight to their face, such as making threats and name calling.
2) Behind their backs, for example, spreading rumours or playing practical jokes.
3) Physical, including pushing, hitting, or slapping.
4) Cyberbullying, for example, trawling over social media.

Bullying can involve a group or an individual exerting their power or perceived power over an individual or multiple people who feel helpless to stop it. Bullying among teens can be difficult to spot as adolescent bullying is usually less physical and more covert. The victims of bullying may also keep it a secret for a number of reasons, such as not wanting to make things worse by telling on the bullies, feelings of shame, being concerned they will worry and upset you as their parent, or genuinely believing nothing can be done. They may even deny being bullied if you ask them directly.

So, how can you know if your teen is being bullied?

1) *School issues.*
   They refuse to attend school or skip it without you knowing. Their academic performance drops, or they express a dislike or fear of attending school.

2) *Emotional and behavioural signs.*
   They get upset before or after school or want to avoid particular places or people. There are noticeable changes in their mood overall. They become increasingly withdrawn, have lower self-confidence, trouble sleeping, and/or start using alcohol or drugs.

3) *Physical signs.*
   They have bruises or other physical injuries that are unexplained, have belongings that are damaged or missing, and regularly tell you they are ill.

There are steps you and your teen can take to address the bullying and help keep your teen safe:

1) *Ignore the bully.*
   Bullies want a response, and the behaviour will continue if they get one. It might be difficult, but have your teen completely ignore the bully and walk away if possible.

2) *Use assertive body language.*
   Tell them to hold their head up high, their shoulders back, and stand tall. This position exudes self-confidence, and they are less likely to be targeted as bullies like vulnerable people.

3) *Tell them to stop.*
   Use a strong, confident voice and address the bully directly. Say, "Stop," or "I don't care what you think."

4) Avoid the bully.

Try to avoid areas that are isolated or hidden from view.

5) Stick with a buddy.

Bullies usually target those who are alone. Also, buddies can stand with your teen against the bully by telling them to stop or go away.

6) Gather evidence.

Have them write down who is bullying them, when, where, and what happened, so you have evidence to give the school or, if it escalates, the police.

7) Talk to people they trust.

Encourage them to talk to you, their friends, or teachers about their experiences and feelings. Tell them you believe them and will help. It is so important they feel supported.

8) Find a safe adult they can talk to about anything and who promises to keep their secret if they really don't want you to know something.

Some kids will not seek out help from their parents because they think they will get in trouble, are ashamed, or don't want to worry them. So naming an adult who promises to keep their secret gives your teen an avenue of support no matter the circumstance. Decide on who this person is together. Don't choose a teacher as they will be obligated to tell you.

9) Talk to the school.

Inform them of the situation and ask for a planning meeting to address the bullying. Do this outside of school hours, as your teen may be fearful of repercussions if you're seen.

10) *Question what the bully says rather than just accepting it.*

Help them question it. Is it the bully's opinion or the truth? If it's their opinion, it doesn't matter, if it's the truth, then unpack with your teen why it's upsetting for them. For example, the bully calls them "fatty." Are they overweight? If yes, why does it cause your teen distress to be called fatty? Do they want to lose weight? If no, then who cares what they say!

11) *Help them detach their self-worth from what the bully says or does.*

This will reduce the impact the bullies' words or actions have on your teen, they will be less likely to internalise what the bully says or believe they deserve what happened.

12) *Help your teen to build resilience so the bully has less impact on other areas of their lives.*

Having resilience means your teen will be less impacted by the bullies' actions, bounce back from them faster and be able to segregate the bullying from other areas of their lives.

13) *Improve their assertiveness skills so they can feel confident to address the bully.*

Building your teen's assertiveness will help them stand up to the bully and may stop the behaviour. It will also prevent your teen from lashing out aggressively to defend themselves, which could result in them getting in trouble themselves.

14) *Make sure they know how to protect themselves, particularly if the bullying is physical.*

For example, know where the nearest exit is, make lots of noise, and even learn how to deflect or block physical aggression by attending self-defence classes.

15) *Encourage empathy.*

Help your teen understand their bully is likely having difficulties themselves, and it isn't about them (though this does not excuse the bully's behaviour). Look at the factors below that may cause a teen to bully others.

16) *Engage professional support.*

As bullying can have severe emotional and psychological impacts, strongly consider seeking professional support for your teen. This will enable them to process what's happening for them and reduce any long-term effects of the bullying.

What if Your Teen Is Bullying Others?

Now for a tough conversation. If one in three teens worldwide is being bullied, there are a huge number of teens doing the bullying. With this statistic, there is a chance your teen or one of their friends could be a bully. If your teen's friend is a bully, there is a high likelihood the behaviour will rub off on your teen due to the strong influence peers have during adolescence, so it's worth being aware of.

If you do discover your teen is bullying others, try not to freak out at your teen or immediately blame yourself. There are things you can do. First, let's understand some of the reasons teens bully others. These can be grouped into psychological and emotional factors and social influences.

Psychological and emotional factors:

1) *They lack a well-established identity.*

As they lack strong values and beliefs, they are more easily influenced by others and are less likely to enforce boundaries and stand against bullying behaviours.

2) *They have low self-worth.*

They put others down to make themselves feel better or because of jealousy.

3) *They have poor impulse control.*

They may lash out consistently at someone who annoys them because they lack the ability to maintain self-control.

4) *They have insufficient anger management skills.*

They haven't learned to control their anger properly and express it in the form of verbal or physical aggression towards a specific person or group of people.

5) *They lack empathy.*

They have a limited understanding of and compassion for those who are different from them and believe their behaviour is acceptable.

Social influences:

1) *Peer pressure.*

As we spoke about earlier, a sense of belonging is important to a teen and they may succumb to peer pressure and bully another teen in order to be accepted by or remain in a social group.

2) *Social status for a position of power.*

They may be using fear and intimidation tactics to be seen as popular among their peer group. Note: this would not be a healthy friendship group.

3) *Family role modelling.*

It is a behaviour they have witnessed in the family, either by siblings, parents, or other household or family members, and are imitating it.

4) *They are the victims of bullying themselves.*

They adopt bullying behaviours so as not to be bullied again or to deflect attention away from themselves toward another kid.

Now you know the possible cause of your teen's bullying behaviour, you can address it and provide them with the correct support. The most important thing is not to react and take some time to acknowledge their behaviours and process the information. Only then should you respond.

1) *Get support.*

It is important to seek support from someone you trust. This could be a close friend who will be non-judgemental of both you and your teen. You could also seek professional help from a counsellor or therapist. It can be a difficult and confronting revelation that your teen is engaging in these types of behaviours and you may need assistance addressing them.

2) *If you are co-parenting, make sure you are on the same page.*
It is fundamental you take a united response to the bullying as you will be more successful at addressing it.

3) *Raise your concerns with your teen.*
Choose an appropriate time and place to have an honest and open conversation with your teen about what you have heard regarding their bullying behaviour. Use the approach described in Chapter 8 on conflict and constructive communication. Explain what you have heard without accusing them, and give them the opportunity to tell their side of the story. They may deny the accusations, admit to them, or explain their behaviours. Their response will influence the way you address the problem.

4) *Condemn the behaviour.*

Separate your teen from the behaviour and express your disapproval of it, explaining it is never right to hurt someone, no matter your reason, and it is unacceptable in your family.

5) *Educate your teen on bullying.*

Explain what bullying is, the different forms it takes, and the detrimental impacts it can have on their victims. They may not realise how bad it actually is.

6) *They have a choice.*

Tell your teen they have a choice not to bully someone and can stop it at any time. They're responsible for their own actions.

7) *Give them consequences for their behaviour.*

Understand these are consequences and not punishments. They must be age-appropriate and proportionate to their actions. Depending on your teen's developmental stage, you could ask them what they think are appropriate and fair consequences of their behaviour. For example, do an anger management course, donate to a charity against bullying, and apologise to the person they have bullied if suitable. They need to be genuinely remorseful for their actions before apologising, and their victim needs to be open to it.

8) *Help them improve their soft skills.*

Teach them to manage their anger better, improve their impulse control, identify and process their feelings (Chapter 6), and communicate better (Chapter 8).

9) *Strengthen their sense of identity.*

Help them figure out who they are and form a strong set of values and beliefs they can align their behaviours with and stand for. They'll have stronger boundaries and be less vulnerable to peer pressure.

10) *Support them to have friends who are a positive influence on them.*
They can meet like-minded teens through community youth groups, sports and arts clubs, or through other activities they enjoy or wish to try.

11) *Engage a coach, mentor, or therapist.*
It is important for your teen to have someone they trust and can rely on outside of the home. Find someone your teen relates to who can support them through challenging times and teach them the life skills they need to succeed.

12) *Be a role model.*
Role model what appropriate social relationships, meaningful friendships, and supportive connections look like. Take time to bond with your teen and show them what it feels like to be in a positive relationship.

Bullying is sadly a common occurrence among teens and, as such, is often not treated as seriously as it needs to be. Bullying is abuse and does have long-term detrimental impacts on an adolescent's psychological, emotional, and physical well-being. It can even lead to suicide. It is difficult to hear if your teen is being bullied or they are exhibiting bullying behaviours, but by utilising the tips above, you can support your teen through this challenging experience.

Romantic and Sexual Relationships

In the context of their teens, sex and romantic relationships can be a challenging and confronting topic for some parents. Each situation is unique, and you must consider your own values and beliefs around sex in relation to what I am about to discuss. I'm not going to mention variables such as religion or culture here as it is too complex.

It is normal and healthy for teens to begin socialising with mixed-sex friendship groups from middle adolescence and to start exploring couplehood. The age and rate at which this happens can vary greatly from teen to teen, so it is best to have age-appropriate conversations around relationships, boundaries, consent, and safe sex earlier on and to normalise discussing these topics through shorter, more frequent conversations. Don't talk to your teen about everything at once, as you will overwhelm them. Although it might be tempting to avoid what can be embarrassing conversations, studies reveal teens who talk to their parents about sex and reproductive health make better and safer decisions around sex.

What should you discuss with your teen about sex? Consent, safe sex, and pornography are discussed in depth next, but here are some general things your teen should know:

1) Anatomy and physiology. Your teen should learn about their sexual and reproductive organs and what they do. They should also know about the sexual and reproductive organs of the opposite sex if they are heterosexual.

2) Sexual desires and thoughts during adolescence are a normal part of development and a result of puberty.

3) Masturbation is a natural and safe way to explore what they enjoy sexually.

4) The risks of sexting and the possibility of it being shared. Even apps such as Snapchat don't guarantee protection because the other person can take a screenshot. Yes, your teen will be notified, but what can they do about it then?

5) Sex is one of the most vulnerable acts a person can do and requires a lot of trust. Your teen needs to trust their partner will respect them during any sexual activity and be confident they will stop if asked to. They also need to know their partner will not gossip about their sex life.

6) They should be comfortable talking honestly and openly with their partner about their boundaries, likes, and dislikes. If they can't, they probably aren't ready to have sex, or it's with the wrong person.

7) Due to their prefrontal cortex reaching maturation in their twenties, teens fall in love based on emotions rather than emotions *and* reasoning. Sex releases endorphins and oxytocin, which can lead to them becoming attached to the person they have sex (which is the point). As such, they may think they can engage in "no-strings sex," but in practice, this is unlikely to be the case, especially for girls. These hormones may even lead to a co-dependent relationship or attachment to an unhealthy relationship.

8) If they feel pressured in any way to engage in sexual activity, they are not ready.

9) Have them explore their reasons for wanting to have sex. Perhaps they are valid, and it is the right decision; they may be able to get their needs met in different ways and wait before having sex or discover it's not actually what they want at all.

10) Also, encourage your teen to reflect on their values. Does having sex align with them?

11) Discuss other forms of physical intimacy and fun ways to connect with their partner that don't involve sex, such as massages, body painting, or nude drawing.

12) Sex can make them body conscious because they are literally exposing themselves to another person. It can also have a detrimental impact on their body image if their partner criticises their body. Though, the opposite is also true if their partner is complimentary of it.

13) Explain sex is not like the movies portray and is likely to be awkward, embarrassing, and messy at first.

14) Your teen needs to be prepared for what might happen after sex. It may not go as they hope. For example, the other person might break up with them, ghost them, or talk about what happened to their friends.

15) Also, explain that sex can be a beautiful, fun, and pleasurable experience when shared with the right person at the right time. It can be a special way to connect deeply with another person and has many other physical and emotional benefits.

Consent

Consent is the agreement to do something or for something to happen. The age of consent is the minimum age a person is deemed legally competent to consent to sexual activities. Under this age, you cannot legally consent and may be prosecuted for engaging in sexual activities. The age of consent varies worldwide from 12 to 21 years old, with some countries outlawing premarital sex and others having no age restriction within marital relationships. Please educate yourself and your teen on the laws in your country or state.

Sex includes all sexual activities, not just sexual intercourse or penetrative sex. These include kissing, fondling, stimulation of the body's erogenous zones, oral sex, fingering/digital penetration of the vagina or anus, hand jobs, and use of sex toys. Due to the varying laws, I shall not speak anymore to the legalities of consent or sex in terms of religion, however, I will discuss what your teen needs to know about consent in order to stay safe.

1) Your teen's body is their body, and no one has the right to touch it or do anything to it they do not want done.
2) They have the right to refuse any sexual act to which they are not comfortable without any explanation.
3) Consent needs to be given clearly and explicitly, otherwise, it is not consent. Your teen needs to say "yes," or even better, "I consent." Consent needs to be asked for and not just given. Teach your teen to ask the person for their consent, not simply expect them to give it. If your teen is unsure about giving consent or whether they have received it from the other person, don't continue.

4) Consent is not a one-time thing. Your teen can consent at the start of a sexual activity and withdraw it at any point during the act. They can consent to one act and not another. They can consent one day and not consent the next. Consent needs to be given every single time they engage in any sexual act and throughout.

5) Your teen cannot consent if they are under the influence of substances such as drugs or alcohol, even if they believe they are able to. They do not have the capacity to make an informed decision to have sex in the first place, and they may be too incapacitated to withdraw consent or communicate their wishes to do so clearly. For example, they are slurring their words. Being under the influence of substances also lowers inhibitions, so your teen may agree to something they would not normally agree to and regret it the next day.

6) The more well-developed your teen's identity, the more they will respect their own bodies and the bodies of others, they will have stronger boundaries and the confidence to express what they do or do not want sexually.

7) Many teens engage in sexual activities because of peer pressure, pressure from their partners, or fear of being judged for not doing them. If your teen has a well established identity, they will also be less vulnerable to submitting under pressure.

8) Have open and honest conversations with your teen about sex and relationships so they will come to you when they have questions, are feeling pressured to engage in sexual activities, or something happens.

Safe Sex

If your teen has unprotected sex, they risk pregnancy and getting sexually transmitted diseases (STDs). They need to know what this means in practice and the potential long-term implications of having unsafe sex.

STDs

The facts:

1) STDs, also called sexually transmitted infections (STIs), are prevalent, with about one in four teenagers contracting an STD every year. They are more likely to catch one than adults are.
2) STDs are infections spread through sexual intercourse (vaginal, anal, or oral) or skin-to-skin sexual contact.
3) Only abstinence can guarantee an STD won't be caught.
4) Condoms, for males and females, are the only form of contraception that can help prevent most STDs.
5) The only way to know if someone has an STD is to be tested, so your teen should be tested regularly once they start having sex, especially if they have multiple partners or change partners.
6) STDs can have unpleasant symptoms or none at all.
7) Some STDs can damage the reproductive organs and cause infertility if left untreated, such as chlamydia and gonorrhoea.
8) Some STDs can be cured while others can't, such as herpes, however, medications can treat the symptoms.
9) Females are more prone physiologically to STDs than males.
10) Your teen can see their own doctor or attend a sexual health clinic, family planning clinic, or women's health centre to get tested and treated for an STD, and at some youth centres.
11) Encourage your teen to talk to you if they suspect they have an STD, but if they really don't want to, identify another safe adult or, depending on their age, they can get tested and treated for STDs without your knowledge. Although it isn't ideal, it is better for them to get tested alone (or with a friend) than not at all because they feel embarrassed, ashamed, or worried about your reaction.

The most common STDs in teens are:

- *Chlamydia*

  It usually has no symptoms, but if there are any, they include discharge from the vagina, penis, or anus; pain in the lower belly; pain during urination, and fever.

  It is treated with antibiotics.

- *Gonorrhea*

  Often there are no symptoms, but if there are, these include discharge from the vagina, penis, or anus; pain in the lower belly and while urinating; pain in testicles for males and bleeding between periods in females; and pain in the rectum.

  It is treated with antibiotics.

- *Syphilis*

  Syphilis has a number of stages and symptoms that get progressively worse. They can show up months after infection and last for years. In the primary stage, symptoms are typically sores on the genitals and rashes on the hands and feet. When it reaches the later stages, syphilis can have devastating effects such as blindness, paralysis, brain damage, and even death. It is treated with antibiotics.

- *Herpes simplex virus (HSV) or genital herpes*

  People who have the disease usually don't have symptoms but can have "outbreaks" of sores around the genitals or anus, which clear within a few weeks.

There is no cure, but medication can be taken to manage the outbreaks and reduce the risk of spreading it.

- *Human papillomavirus (HPV)*

  HPV causes genital warts, which usually appear within a few months of infection, though not everyone with HPV develops them. HPV usually goes away on its own after about two years. There is a vaccine for HPV which prevents infection.

Other STDs include pelvic inflammatory disease (PID), HIV and AIDS, pubic lice, and trichomoniasis (trich). There is a wealth of information on the internet about STDs, and your local medical providers will be happy to speak to your teen about them in detail.

If your teen believes they have an STD or may have been exposed to one, or you have noticed any suspicious symptoms, they must get tested immediately and abstain from sex until they receive their results. The next course of action will be determined by whether they are positive or negative and the STD they have contracted. Their medical providers will give them clear directions on the next steps.

Although it will be embarrassing, they will need to inform any sexual partners if they have tested positive. But if they are mature enough to have sex, they should be mature enough to have adult conversations about it. If they are adamant about not speaking to their current or prior partners, there are apps that can do this anonymously.

The strongest message your teen needs to know is that by having sex (even safe sex), they risk getting an STD and must get tested regularly.

Teenage Pregnancy

Teens are extremely fertile, with the chances of becoming pregnant in a given year being about 90%. Women are fertile 6 to 8 days around ovulation, but as teens have irregular periods, it is more difficult to predict when they are ovulating. With these statistics, it's clear how a little carelessness can carry a high risk of pregnancy.

Although it is possible for teens to have healthy pregnancies and be great parents, many experience a number of stressors and challenges both during pregnancy and after the birth. These include:

1) Health risks for the mother during pregnancy.
2) Health risks for the baby during pregnancy.
3) Risks for both mother and baby during birth.
4) Pressures on the relationship between the teen parents both during the pregnancy and after the baby is born.
5) Often, the father is absent, so the mother is a single parent.
6) Relationship issues with their parents and extended families.
7) Friendships may be challenged and/or lost. They will certainly change.
8) They won't be able to do "normal" teen things.
9) Disruption to education and work.
10) Teen parents have been linked to increased use of alcohol.
11) Higher risk of postpartum depression for the mother.
12) Financial burdens of raising a child.
13) Increased risk of long-term poverty.
14) Implications if their religion or culture frowns upon unwed sex and children out of wedlock.
15) If the parents choose not to continue the pregnancy and abort it, there are potential physical risks for the girl. An abortion will also likely have emotional and psychological consequences for both teens.

16) Giving the baby up for adoption can also lead to huge emotional and psychological challenges for both teens.

17) Due to the multiple stressors teen parents can face and their developmental stage, meaning they are less able to manage their emotions, babies are at a higher risk of harm.

Contraception

Boys are easier when it comes to contraception as they currently have the choice of condoms and a vasectomy, which I obviously wouldn't recommend at their age. Girls have a lot more options. If you have a daughter, I'd suggest you take her to the doctor or sexual health clinic to discuss her options for contraception, including female condoms and the sponge (both hormone free), the implant, pills, injections, an intrauterine device (IUD), vaginal rings and skin patches (hormone methods). They each have their advantages and disadvantages, so she needs all the information to make an informed decision. You can tell her your opinion, but allow her, under her doctor's advice, to have autonomy over her own body and trust her to make the right choice. It will empower her to make other positive decisions for her body and well-being.

Have the conversation with both sexes about the importance of using condoms to prevent unwanted pregnancy and as protection against sexually transmitted diseases. They need to know using contraception isn't 'uncool' or embarrassing but shows respect for their body, their future, and those of their partner.

Pornography

Pornography is sexual subject matter in text, picture, or video format that is sexually arousing. It is designed for adult use. However, many teens have seen it either by accident or on purpose. Adult blocks on porn sites or their devices do not completely prevent teens from accessing porn.

It is difficult to know exactly how many teens have seen porn as it relies largely on self-reported data. However, a recent survey of 1,300 teens by Common Sense Media in the U.S. (Teens and Pornography, 2022) revealed some startling data. The average age of teens viewing porn for the first time in the U.S. was 12 years old. Three out of four respondents had seen porn. Of those who had seen porn, 44 % had seen it intentionally, and 58% accidentally (including those who had both seen it accidentally and intentionally). The most troubling for me is that 45% said they believe online porn gives helpful information about sexual relationships. It is clearly extremely difficult to prevent your teen from seeing porn altogether, either by choice or accidentally.

So what can you do? Talk to your teen about porn when you believe it is appropriate, which is probably sooner than you think. I'm hesitant to give an age because every teen develops at a different rate, and what might be an appropriate age for one teen may not be for another. I would suggest including porn in the conversations you have with them around sex.

Why is porn such an issue for teens?

1) *Teens see porn as a way to learn about themselves.*
   Teens report using it to discover what sexual acts aroused them (physiological response) and what turns them on (mental aspect). The acts depicted in porn are usually more extreme than those of mainstream society.

2) *Feelings of guilt and shame.*
   Negative emotions such as guilt and shame are felt by many teens who watch porn, which can result in them associating these feelings with sex itself, which can be harmful to their sexual relationships.

3) *Unrealistic sexual relationships.*

   In reality, sexual relationships just aren't like those depicted in porn. And for your teen to expect them to be will result in unfulfilled sexual relationships.

4) *Violence and aggression.*

   Porn exposes teens to sex scenes depicting acts such as choking, slapping, rape, or a person being in pain.

5) *Lack of consent.*

   Consent is rarely given in mainstream pornography.

6) *It rarely shows the use of contraception.*

   This makes it seem normal and acceptable not to use condoms.

7) *Stereotypes.*

   Porn represents people from certain races and ethnic backgrounds in stereotypical ways. This can be harmful to the identities of teens from these races and ethnicities.

8) *Negative representation of women.*

   Women are often objectified in porn and used only for a man's sexual pleasure.

9) *Addiction.*

   Teens are more vulnerable to forming an addiction to porn due to their developmental stage. This can have detrimental impacts on their emotional, psychological, social, and physiological well-being (I shall discuss addiction in depth in Chapter 4).

10) *Child Pornography.*

   Sites such as Pornhub have even been found to contain videos of child pornography.

Talk to your teen about these harmful aspects of porn and ask what their thoughts are about these issues, as it is likely your teen was unaware of them. By having open conversations about sex and relationships, you can help them build a healthy narrative around sex and have a positive and realistic view of it. If you believe your teen has an issue with porn and are concerned, I strongly recommend seeking professional help from a therapist.

Case Study: Cassie, 16 years.
(name changed for confidentiality)

The Struggle

Cassie was raised by her foster father after he divorced his wife and she moved away. Cassie was close to her father when she was younger, so she chose to remain with him. As she got older and became an adolescent, their relationship started to break down. Cassie no longer talked to him about important topics; her father seriously struggled with her behaviour. Cassie was regularly skipping school and hanging out with the wrong crowd. She'd been sexually active since she was 14 years old and currently had a boyfriend with whom she was having sex and sending nude photos on Snapchat.

The Transformation

I worked on conflict and constructive communication with both Cassie and her father so they could reconnect and start to rebuild their relationship. Cassie opened up about why she skipped school, telling her father she was struggling with the content and didn't enjoy it. She wanted to leave school to study childcare.

I assisted Cassie in applying to TAFE (Technical and Further Education, a vocational education provider in Australia) to get her certificate in early learning and find a nearby childcare centre to do her placement. Cassie started socialising with the other students and childcare staff, cutting ties with her old friendship group. I supported Cassie's father to have open and honest conversations with her about sex, as awkward as he found it. Cassie attended a sexual health clinic for contraceptive advice, deciding on the implant because she thought she'd forget the pill or injection. Cassie was really appreciative and surprised by her father's new approach and was more inclined to talk to him about things other than just sex.

I helped educate both Cassie and her father on consent and the dangers of sending nude photos, even over Snapchat, as, although the photos disappear, the person can take a screenshot of it. Snapchat will notify Cassie, but there's nothing she can do about it then. And despite Cassie and her boyfriend having a good relationship at the time, I had seen things turn nasty with exes showing their friends the nude photos, spreading them around the school, or even posting them online. Finally, I told Cassie that it is illegal in Australia to take, keep, share, or send any sexual images or videos of someone under 18 as it constitutes child pornography. Cassie was horrified at this and said she had no idea. She told her boyfriend, and they stopped exchanging photos.

Conclusion

Relationships and a sense of belonging are extremely important to a person's well-being, especially during adolescence. Teens have a natural instinct to pull away from their parents and strengthen connections with their friends to explore their identity. It is important for you, as their parent, to find the balance between encouraging them to seek their independence and providing a stable home they can return to when they need to.

If your teen has the skills to form and maintain healthy friendships, they will have higher levels of self-esteem, be less likely to engage in risky and addictive behaviours, or develop mental health illnesses. Your teen is more likely to make better and safer decisions when it comes to sex if they have positive friendships, emotional support, and a well-developed identity. They are also more likely to choose good partners and have healthy relationships with stronger boundaries, raising issues within the dynamic as they occur and walking away from toxic relationships.

CHAPTER 4

The Attraction to Addiction

"Substance misuse isn't the real problem,
it's the 'why' you need to worry about."

Addiction is an intense and inescapable physiological and/or psychological urge to take or do something for the immediate reward, regardless of any harmful consequences. Addiction is a chronic condition, the behaviour is compulsive, and the person with the addiction has an inability to stop the behaviour. It is, however, treatable.

The adolescent stage makes teens especially vulnerable to addiction, and they have a greater chance of it developing into a long-term issue. As we discussed in Section 1, a teen's propensity for risk-taking and thrill-seeking is higher due to their underdeveloped brain. As their prefrontal cortex is not yet mature, their judgement, decision-making, planning, and impulse control are impeded. Teens also have a higher reliance on the amygdala for decision-making than adults, which is responsible for emotions and impulsivity. An adolescent's brain also has an increased sensitivity to dopamine, which is part of the reward circuit and drives, focuses, and motivates your teen. As such, they are more inclined to experiment with substances such as nicotine, alcohol, and drugs, which give them a "hit" of the feel-good hormone dopamine. Dopamine levels in the body then drop and remain at a decreased level for a while, resulting in feelings of sadness and a low mood. To feel good again, the teen will re-engage in the behaviour that produced the initial high, causing them to be caught in a cycle of use and potentially develop an addiction.

Teens are also susceptible to becoming addicted to anything else that gives them the "feel good high" produced by the release of dopamine and endorphins, such as social media, video games, food, and exercise. Addictions can co-occur, meaning if your teen has one addiction, they are susceptible to having others. They are also likely to replace one addiction with another if the underlying reason for their behaviour is not addressed.

Due to the very important developmental stage teens are in, addiction to substances such as drugs, nicotine, and alcohol can result in long-term psychological, physiological, and emotional damage—it can impact them socially and have detrimental effects on their academic performance. It is, therefore, an extremely serious issue and one you must be aware of as a parent of a teenager so you can prevent them from developing an addiction in the first place or address it early on if they do.

Furthermore, understanding addiction can help you understand your teen's behaviour in a different light and know they aren't "just being bad and need to stop," but instead, there are a number of factors and complex issues at play which need to be considered and managed appropriately. It is difficult to determine why one teen develops an addiction while another does not. However, there are factors that have been identified as increasing a teen's likelihood of forming an addiction. I've grouped them under six main categories.

1) Biological factors.

   a) *Brain development.* As just discussed, a teen's brain is not fully matured. They are more likely to take substances and engage in

70

addictive activities regardless of the consequences and are more susceptible to becoming addicted to them.

b) *Genetic predisposition.* Genetic makeup has been identified as contributing between 40 % to 60 % of a person's risk factor for developing a wide range of addictions.

2) Emotional factors.

a) *They lack emotional regulation.* Teens take drugs to manage strong emotions they cannot regulate themselves or escape feelings they find uncomfortable.

3) Psychological factors.

a) *Mental health issues.* Teens may self-medicate with substances to alleviate mental health symptoms.

b) *Trauma.* Trauma and substance abuse often co-occur as it provides an escape from the effects of the trauma.

4) Social factors.

a) *Peers and friends engage in addictive behaviours together.* Teens may feel peer pressure to take substances or engage in certain activities. Also, these behaviours can be normalised if a teen's social group is doing them.

b) *Started at a younger age.* The younger a teen starts taking substances, the more likely they are to become addicted.

c) *Negative role modelling.* They see adults around them role-modelling behaviours such as drinking and taking drugs and copy them.

d) *Low school achievement.* Poor academic performance has been linked to increased risks of drug and alcohol use in teens.

e) *Social isolation.* A sense of belonging is fundamental to a teen's identity and well-being; therefore, social isolation makes them vulnerable to addiction.

5) Environmental factors.

a) *A lack of parental supervision.* Teens without adequate supervision have the opportunity to take substances and engage in addictive behaviour.

b) *Parents are addicts.* Teens raised in a home where substances are taken by their parents normalises the behaviour.

c) *Accessibility to a substance or the activity.* The more accessible a substance is to a teen, the more likely they are to take it.

d) *Abusive or neglectful home environment.* Being raised in a home where there is abuse or neglect makes the teen much more vulnerable to taking drugs and/or alcohol and developing addictions.

e) *Unstable family dynamic.* If there is a lot of conflict at home or instability, teens may turn to substances or activities that bring comfort and relief from the situation.

f) *Poverty.* Research has shown that living in poverty increases an adolescent's likelihood of substance misuse.

6) Personality traits. Researchers have identified six personality traits common to people with addictions. Many of these are adolescent characteristics, explaining why teens are especially vulnerable to addiction.

a) Impulsivity.

b) Low self-esteem.

c) Compulsivity.

d) Nonconformity.

e) Grandiosity.

f) Inability to handle stress.

Despite these risk factors, there are protective factors you can put in place to prevent your teen from engaging in substance misuse and compulsive behaviours. These include:

1) *A well developed identity.*

   If your teen has a well developed identity, they have higher levels of self-respect, strong values and beliefs, all of which make them less inclined to engage in substance misuse or ongoing behaviours resulting in addiction.

2) *Emotional regulation.*

   A teen's ability to regulate their emotions more effectively means they do not use unhealthy ways to manage their emotions.

3) *Positive relationships.*

   Teens with strong and supportive relationships with family and friends have a sense of belonging and safe people to turn to when they need it.

4) *Positive role models.*

   Teens exposed to adults who role model positive and healthy behaviours are more inclined to imitate the behaviour.

5) *A stable home environment.*

   A safe and secure home environment provides teens with a space to feel grounded and protected when things get challenging.

6) *Interests and hobbies.*

Having something else to focus on and keep them busy means teens are less likely to form addictions to unhealthy activities.

7) *Physical activities.*

Teens engaging in sport or physical activities are less likely to put toxic substances into their bodies, as they have a greater respect for their health.

8) *Goals.*

Teens with aspirations and goals they are working towards are more focused on the future and have a positive attitude about it, meaning they won't engage in activities that may interfere with their success.

9) *Academic engagement.*

Teens who are performing well at school and/or are engaged with school are less likely to undermine their achievements by taking substances or engaging in compulsive behaviours.

10) *Guidelines and boundaries.*

Teens who have guidelines and boundaries are more able to make decisions in light of these restrictions and reflect on the possible consequences of breaking them compared to teens who are allowed to do whatever they want.

11) *Open and constructive communication.*

Teens who are able to communicate about their feelings and challenges effectively are able to process and manage them more healthily.

The most common forms of addiction in teens are screens, in particular, gaming and social media; cigarettes and vaping; alcohol and recreational drugs, with food and exercise addiction becoming increasingly more concerning. I shall discuss addiction in relation to each of these.

Excessive Screen Time

Screen time is, in itself, not an issue. Problems arise when it is excessive, and the content is inappropriate for the age or individual. For example, a 13-year-old playing violent video games rated for 16 or 18-year-olds is inappropriate because the violence is more graphic and realistic.

So, what does screen time actually mean? It includes any activity done on a digital screen, such as:

1) Watching television.
2) Engaging with social media and other apps on mobile phones.
3) Streaming content on tablets.
4) Playing video games.
5) Reading ebooks on an e-reader.
6) Doing school work on computers.
7) Using Google and other search engines to look up information.
8) Virtual reality (VR) devices.
9) Watching movies at the cinema.
10) Playing educational media games.

So, how much screen time is too much? There has been a lot of research into the effects of screen time on adolescents and when these effects become harmful. Studies have reported teens averaging between 7.5 and 9 hours of screen time a day, with boys spending more time on it than girls. Girls are more likely to spend time on social media, while boys use it for gaming. The recommended sedentary recreational use for teens is 2 hours, so it excludes school work. However, there are multiple factors to consider when deciding how much screen time is too much for your teen, as it may be better for them to have less than the recommended 2 hours.

Research such as the Adolescent Brain Cognitive Development Study in the U.S., a global study led by the University of Queensland on screen time;

reports by Common Sense Media, and other reputable studies have shown excessive screen time may have the following effects on your teen:

1) They have a reduction in social skills due to limited person-to-person interactions because your teen isn't practising their social skills or aren't learning them in the first place.

2) Your teen may develop social anxiety due to engaging in fewer social events and interactions.

3) Compulsive use gets in the way of them doing other things.

4) Too much screen time can cause overstimulation and hyperarousal due to the speed at which the information is presented and processed.

5) Overstimulation, in turn, can lead to poor focus and mental fatigue, which may result in your teen having disrupted behaviour and outbursts.

6) It may impact brain development and sensory processing due to the fundamental developmental stage your teen is in. This includes emotional development.

7) It can increase feelings of loneliness as your teen is literally alone or choosing screens over social interactions and face-to-face time with their friends.

8) It is associated with increased symptoms of depression and anxiety, particularly if your teen is already vulnerable to mental health challenges.

9) They may have trouble sleeping due to artificial blue light from the screens and excessive brain stimulation, making it harder to switch off.

10) Lack of sleep has a negative ripple effect on many other areas of their well-being, such as mood, academic performance, and food choices.

11) There's an increased chance of your teen being overweight or obese due to their limited physical activity and increased snacking often associated with screen time.

12) Less physical activity also impacts the subsequent beneficial side effects it has, such as physical fitness, cardio health, and better mental health.

13) Digital eye strain and possible headaches from staring at a screen for extended periods.

14) Bad posture and neck tension from sitting too long or looking down at screens.

However, I do not suggest you immediately cut screen time to 2 hours. If it is an addiction, going cold turkey can have problematic outcomes, and your teen will react extremely poorly to it. Instead, collaborate on guidelines around screen time for everyone (refer to the previous activity on setting household boundaries in Chapter 3, under "The Family") and get on board with your teen to role model positive behaviour around screen time. It will also benefit you and your relationship with your teen.

Ask your teen their opinion about their screen time. What do they think it includes? How much time do they think they spend on screens? And how much of this time do they actually enjoy and consciously engage in?

Here are some suggestions to help reduce screen time:

1) *Track screen time.* Your teen probably doesn't even know how much screen time they actually have. They can use tracking apps on phones, which also break down what they are doing during their screen time. They will need to track other activities manually, such as TV and gaming.

2) *Screen downtime.* They can set a downtime on their phone, which shuts down the app either at a certain time or after a period of use. Although these can be overridden, it makes them consciously think about going on the app.

3) *Delete some apps.* They can still access their accounts, but will need to go through a search engine and sign in rather than just click on an app.

4) *Schedule screen use and time.* Schedule certain times that work well for them and your family, ensuring it doesn't get in the way of more important things, for example, after homework is done.

5) *Turn off notifications.* It is extremely difficult to ignore notifications, meaning your teen may be constantly checking their phone as soon as the beep alerts them to something new. By switching off notifications on at least some of their apps, they will reduce the frequency at which they are checking their phones.

6) *No screens 60 minutes before bed or after waking.* Screens have a negative impact on sleep, so putting guidelines around nighttime and morning use helps reduce sleep disruption.

7) *Screens outside of the bedroom* to reduce temptation. Get digital alarm clocks for the time and an alarm.

8) *Only one screen at a time.* If your teen is on their phone, then switch off the TV. They only have one set of eyes, so focus on one screen.

9) *Get a smartwatch.* Although it sounds counterintuitive because a smartwatch is technically a screen, having one has been proven to reduce screen time because you pick up your phone less and, therefore, scroll less, reducing incidental use.

Try one or two of these suggestions at first, and once your teen has become used to the new norm, introduce others. And get on board! Not only would you benefit from reducing your screen time, but your teen would also be more inclined to embrace the process as you will be doing it together and leading by example.

Social Media

Social media is the collective term for integrated digital technology, such as websites and applications, that enable the creation and sharing of information and the active participation in social networks and communities.

Various surveys and studies have reported approximately 90 to 97 % of teens have some form of social media account. The most popular social media platforms among teenagers at the time of writing this book are TikTok, Snapchat, YouTube, and Instagram, with Facebook losing popularity. With the existence of smartphones, these applications are literally available at our fingertips, and many teens report using social media "constantly." Social media has both pros and cons for your teen, depending on a number of factors, including the ways they use it and the extent to which they are on it. We covered screen time previously, so these are specific to social media use.

The Unhealthy Side of Social Media

Social media can be detrimental to your teen's well-being if used constantly and if your teen doesn't have a well-developed identity.

1) *Fake or real.*
   With the current technology, influencers are able to modify photos and videos, so it is difficult to know what is actually real. People can change their bodies, faces, background scenery, and present a fictional image as reality. Now, the image may even be completely AI-generated.

2) *The comparison trap.*
   They compare their own life to the unrealistic presentation of other people's lives on social media.

3) *Increase materialism.*

Your teen sees what the rich and famous have and covert their lifestyle and belongings.

4) *Perfectionism.*

They only see the final perfect product that someone posts rather than all the failures, takes, and edits that happened before. This can result in your teen having unrealistic expectations and negative feelings about themselves when they do not do things perfectly the first time.

5) *Negative comments.*

Social media exposes your teen to possible trawling and online bullying, which can negatively impact their mental health and self-esteem.

6) *Immediacy.*

Social media is at their fingertips and always accessible, which feeds the need for immediacy rather than understanding the satisfaction of delayed gratification.

7) *FOMO, fear of missing out.*

Teenagers are able to see what others are doing because they post real-time updates online. So if they're not invited to an event or party, for example, they feel left out and even rejected.

8) *Social validation.*

Your teen may seek social validation through the amount of ticks and comments they receive, which can result in their self-esteem being tied to how many they get on any given post.

9) *Spread of misinformation.*

Social media can present information as the truth when it is not, which can be dangerous when the information is hateful or harmful to a particular demographic.

10) *Distraction.*

Your teen may use it to distract themselves from challenging situations or tasks they don't want to do.

11) *Body image issues.*

Your teen may develop a negative body image from receiving critical comments about theirs from other people or from comparing themselves to others on social media who have the "ideal" body (which we know doesn't exist). They can also receive indirect messages about their body, for example, through other people being "fat shamed."

12) *Used to numb emotions to escape uncomfortable feelings.*

Your teen may use social media as a distraction when they experience difficult feelings rather than process them.

13) *Constant access to information.*

It impacts sleep and functioning due to overstimulation.

14) *Impacts mental health.*

Many of the cons of social media discussed above, individually or in combination, can impact your teen's mental health.

Activity: Watch *The Social Dilemma* on Netflix as a family and discuss your thoughts about it.

The Benefits of Social Media

However, I don't suggest you stop your teen from using social media altogether because, if used correctly and intentionally, it can be a positive addition to your teen's life in a number of ways.

1) *Self-expression.*

Social media gives your teen the platform to express themselves freely through videos, photos, and text.

2) *Connection.*

It is a way for them to connect with their friends and to form friendships with those they wouldn't in real life because of factors such as location, different backgrounds, and mixing in separate social circles.

3) *Belonging.*

They can find a sense of belonging by forming friendships with others like them. This is particularly important for teens who are in a minority, feel isolated, or misunderstood by those around them.

4) *Inspiration.*

There are many people and pages who can be hugely inspirational to your teen, unlocking their creativity.

5) *Motivational.*

There are also many people posting motivational quotes and videos, boosting your teen's drive and productivity.

6) *Social validation.*

Although social validation can be negative if their self-esteem is attached to it, it can also be positive if it helps your teen understand where they are and how they can improve.

7) *Entertaining.*

Social media can be a source of fun and entertainment for your teen that elicits good feelings.

8) *Educational.*

There is a lot of educational material, pages, and profiles that your teen can engage with.

9) *Personal development.*

The combination of inspiring, motivational, and educational posts and social validation can drive your teens to improve themselves.

So, how can you help your teen use social media in healthy and positive ways?

Suggest these to your teen and ask what they think of the ideas. Don't impose them as rules upon your teen, or they will not have the positive impact they're designed to.

1) Recommend your teen actively engage with the post instead of passively looking at it. Think about the post. What do they like or dislike about it? Does it resonate? Then, if they feel aligned, they can leave a positive comment, ask a constructive question, or put an emoji.

2) Have them critique the post as they look at it rather than taking it at face value. For example, has the image been edited, or is the person who they say they are, and is the information they share credible?

3) Suggest when they look at a post or a person's page to reflect on how they feel and why. Does it elicit positive or negative feelings?

4) Have your teen redefine what an influencer is. Many social media influencers followed by teens are famous singers or actors, dancers, stylists, and makeup artists. They are people who largely focus on their appearance, material gain, or status. Instead, I recommend they also follow people because they stand for something and have a message. Of course, some famous actors and influencers do!

5) Encourage your teen to follow a more diverse range of people. For example, they might follow those who have a different gender

identity, sexuality, body shape, race, religion, nationality, physical ability, socioeconomic status, or background. These people might not fit the unrealistic and normative beauty standards set by society. Immersing themselves in such diversity helps your teen understand that difference is something to be celebrated.

6) Do a social media account cleanse. If they don't feel good, inspired, or gain some level of new understanding, knowledge, or insight from following someone, they should unfollow that person or page.

Activity: Try a family media detox. Social media is only one form of media. We largely underestimate the impact media has on our well-being and that of our teens. Media messages are constantly washing over our brains through the TV, radio, newspapers, magazines, the internet, and our phones with compounding effects. Do a family media detox by cutting out all media. Try it just for a day and see how you go; you might want to do more!

I know suggesting a media detox will likely cause you anxiety, let alone your teen, but trust me, it will have positive impacts for both you and them in a number of ways. Here are some benefits of reducing your teens' exposure to the media:

1) *Improved self-esteem.*

The media displays society's ideas of what the perfect male and, in particular, the ideal female looks like. Magazines, social media, television shows, and movies all contain often unattainable representations of men and women as the norm. These distorted ideals are especially dangerous to extremely impressionable and vulnerable teens who compare themselves to and fall drastically short of these men and women. Although it is natural for teens to compare themselves to others, by cutting out their exposure to media, they will engage in a more healthy form of comparison against other "normal" teenagers.

2) *Better mental health.*
Media feeds off the negativity bias, a natural tendency for people to pay more attention to bad news. These days, news on television and radio can be easily accessed via mobile devices, and it's on our social media feeds. Researchers found the news causes stress and feelings of anxiety, so reducing your teen's exposure to it can positively impact their mental health.

3) *Enhanced relationships.*
Your teen will have more free time to engage in real-life relationships with family and friends. With less distraction, they will also be more present during these interactions and able to connect at a deeper level.

4) *Engage in new activities.*
They will have to find other activities to keep themselves occupied, such as hobbies, sport, board games, or music.

5) *Boredom leads to creativity.*
It's been specifically proven that boredom helps stimulate creativity. So, without media to keep them occupied, your teen will likely be more creative and productive.

Gaming

Like social media, gaming has both pros and cons to it, so with some guidelines, it can be a positive addition to your teen's life.

Pros.

1) *Connection.*

Most games are online and multiplayer, so it is a way for friends to connect without being in the same physical location as other gamers worldwide.

2) *Mental health.*

Gaming can be a way for your teen to relax, destress, and escape from the challenges of life for a bit.

3) *Active participation.*

Depending on the game, they will need to use their fine motor skills, hand-eye coordination, visual perception, memory, problem-solving skills, and collaborative skills if working as a teen.

4) *Improved skills.*

Those who play action games learn new sensory motor skills faster than those who don't. Video games have been shown to improve hand-eye coordination and fine motor skills.

Cons.

1) *Bullying.*

As the majority of games are online, your teen will be exposed to different types of people who may be disrespectful towards them.

2) *Impact self-esteem.*

Your teen's self-esteem can be impacted if they attach their self-worth to winning and losing or don't perform at their best.

3) *Increased anger and aggression.*

Studies have shown violent games are a predictor of aggressive feelings, thoughts, and behaviours in both genders.

4) *Disconnect from real-life relationships.*

If your teen plays a lot of video games, they're engaging less in their friendships and with their family.

5) *Distraction.*

Games can distract them from other important things, such as schoolwork.

6) *Addictive.*

Games are designed to be psychologically addictive. They're an immersive experience and result in high levels of dopamine being produced. Teens will play more to seek out this feel-good rush.

Here are five tips to ensure your teen gets the most out of gaming without negative effects.

1) *Create a gaming plan.*

Collaborate with your teen and create a gaming plan setting limits on when, where, and for how long they can game. Bear in mind that experts advise teens to have 2 hours maximum recreational screen time per day, which includes gaming, social media, online use, and TV. The console can be kept in a communal area so you can monitor your teen's gaming if they are unlikely to adhere to the limits. Gaming could be a weekend-only activity or something they do after homework is completed. Whatever best suits the needs of your teen and family.

2) *Appropriate games.*

Ensure your teen only has access to games appropriate for them. This not only means age-appropriate, but also meets their individual requirements. For example, if your teen gets anxiety, perhaps don't allow them to play horror games where their fight-or-flight flight response is constantly triggered. Also, question the need for violent games. Is there a less violent alternative?

3) *Monitor the impact of gaming.*

Monitor other aspects of your teen's life, or better still, have them monitor them. Include areas such as their sleep, peer relationships, school performance, and mood to see how gaming impacts them. If you have concerns, make adjustments to the gaming plan.

4) *Play with them.*

Gaming with your teen can be fun, help you bond, and provide an opportunity to talk while you play.

5) *Other interests.*

Make sure your teen has other hobbies and interests they enjoy and can do when their gaming time is up. This reduces pushback when their time is over.

Case Study: Jasper, 14 years.
(name changed for confidentiality)

The Struggle

Jasper was constantly gaming and rarely socialised with his friends in real life. He had started to develop social anxiety, was getting aggressive in his communication at home, and verbally threatening his siblings. He was always in his room and rarely had dinner with or spent time with his family. Jasper's school work was getting impacted as he either didn't do it or was unfocused when he did. He was reluctant to attend school and would rush straight home to get on the computer to play his games. Jasper would often 'be sick' and spend the day gaming. Jasper's parents found it easier and less stressful to just let him play.

The Transformation

I educated Jasper and his parents on addiction and explained why he needed to play his games so much and why he could get very angry and upset when he couldn't. They made a gaming plan together, which set boundaries around his gaming. They started off with Jasper being allowed to play for longer periods of time and gradually cutting it to under the recommended 2 hours so he could dedicate screen time to other activities.

We worked on emotional literacy, after which Jasper agreed to play less violent games as he acknowledged he felt more angry and was verbally aggressive after playing them. Jasper also realised he loved the adrenaline he got from fighting and racing games. Jasper started to channel his risk-taking and aggression into other activities, such as boxing and go-karting. He did some of these activities with his family and started to socialise with friends in real life. First, they went to arcades, and as his anxiety eased, he hung out with them in other social situations. Jasper and his family noticed a change in Jasper's behaviour and attitude. He spent more time out of his room and with them, and he went out a lot more with friends. He was more engaged with school and focused on his homework. He chose to do other things besides gaming even when he had the option to play.

Cigarettes and Vaping

It is estimated that worldwide, approximately 24 million teens between the ages of 13 and 15 smoke cigarettes. Although this figure in itself is startling, e-cigarettes and vaping are becoming exponentially more popular among teens. The World Health Organization's Global Youth Tobacco Survey in 2023 reported e-cigarettes used among 12 to 16-year-olds ranged from 3.3 % to 10.8

%. The lowest use was in Southeast Asia and the highest in the Western Pacific. These are huge numbers, considering the detrimental effects vapes have on teens' health.

Cigarettes and roll-your-own tobacco are full of chemicals, with reports stating they contain between 4,000 to more than 7,000 chemicals, with nicotine being the main chemical ingredient, which is extremely addictive.

Nicotine is a stimulant and has immediate pleasing effects on the brain. It also triggers the release of adrenaline, which increases the smoker's blood pressure, heart rate, and breathing and adds to the feel-good sensations. However, these effects are short-lived and result in the urge to have another cigarette to 'feel good' again. The issue with cigarettes is their effect diminishes, so the more you smoke, the more you need to smoke to get the same pleasurable effects the nicotine previously induced. The result is addiction. Nicotine also causes issues with memory, concentration, self-control, attention, and sleep and worsens anxiety and depression. Nicotine also leads to withdrawal symptoms in the form of unpleasant physical and psychological changes when a smoker tries to stop.

Signs to look out for if your teen is smoking cigarettes:

1) The smell of cigarettes on them and their clothing.
2) They have cigarettes and lighters or matches in their possession.
3) They use body spray or other overpowering smells to hide the smell of smoke.
4) They are acting suspiciously and secretively.
5) Their friends smoke.
6) They are coughing, wheezing, or easily out of breath.
7) They show signs of irritability.

E-Cigarettes or vapes are battery-operated aerosol devices that heat a liquid to produce a vapour that users inhale. The first commercially successful e-cigarette was invented in 2003 by a Chinese pharmacist, Hon Lick, after his father died from lung cancer associated with smoking. He had the intention it would help him quit smoking personally, but it didn't. Hon Lick now uses both vapes and cigarettes.

Although vaping is currently thought to be less harmful than smoking, it is still not healthy or risk-free, especially for teenagers:

1) E-cigarettes usually still contain nicotine, meaning they're addictive.
2) Formaldehyde, a cancer-causing chemical, may form if not enough liquid reaches the heating element or the liquid overheats.
3) They may also contain marijuana distillate.
4) When a teen vapes, they are more likely to smoke cigarettes and possibly develop other addictions.
5) There are increased chances of developing chronic bronchitis and causing damage to their lungs, which can ultimately be life-threatening.

With the fruity and juicy flavours available, vapes are particularly appealing to teens, with an overwhelming number of them choosing to use flavoured ones. It is also easier for teens to hide the fact they smoke from their parents because they don't smell of smoke, and they don't need lighters, which are obvious giveaways.

Signs to look out for if your teen is smoking e-cigarettes:

1) E-cigarettes and cartridges may look like USBs.
2) New smells, particularly sweet and fruity ones.
3) The development of health issues such as coughing and wheezing.
4) Your teen is sneaking off or acting suspiciously, like not letting you near their things.
5) You're aware their friends vape, as many teens reported they first vaped with a friend.

6) They are moody and irritable.

If you suspect that your teen is smoking or vaping, what can you do about it?

1) Do you smoke? If so, strongly consider stopping, as you are role-modelling the behaviour and normalising it.
2) Don't react, but take time to process the information and respond appropriately at the right time.
3) Tell your teen you suspect they are smoking and why.
4) Ask them what they understand about smoking, vaping, and the potential dangers.
5) Express your concerns about the harmful effects smoking and vaping may have on them.
6) Discuss addiction. Ask why they started smoking and continue to do so. Do they understand what addiction is and how it works?
7) Help them identify their values. Does smoking align with their values or not?
8) Encourage them to engage in more physical activity.
9) Help them improve their self-esteem and self-respect. They are less likely to want to harm themselves through smoking.
10) Work on their emotional regulation so they don't use smoking as a way to manage difficult feelings (chapter 6).
11) Help them with their constructive communication so they can talk about their problems and feelings instead of smoking when they are stressed or feeling challenged (chapter 8).
12) Assist them in setting healthy boundaries which will act as a protective factor against stress and negative feelings.
13) Suggest they save money for something they really want.
14) Empower them to have conversations with friends about smoking and vaping and why they want to stop or don't want to do it when offered.

15) Find other healthy ways to get "high" and replace the "feel good" feelings they get from smoking like those discussed in Chapter 2.

16) Make a plan to stop smoking or reduce smoking and then stop.

17) Prepare them (and yourself) for withdrawals when they stop.

18) Get help from a mental health professional or addiction specialist.

Alcohol

As a parent, it is unlikely that you can prevent your teen from experimenting with alcohol completely. However, you can instil safer drinking habits in them, which will serve them well into the future. In this discussion, we will cover why teens drink, the effects alcohol has on them during this important stage of development, how to recognize if they are drinking, and the best ways to respond if they are. The good news is that fewer teens are turning to alcohol than in the past. Therefore, it is possible to encourage good habits by setting clear rules around alcohol and expressing your disapproval of underage drinking as early as possible.

The legal age for drinking differs worldwide, ranging from 15 to 25 years old, with the majority of countries setting the age limit at 18 years old. Eleven countries have a complete ban on alcohol. You and your teen must know the legal drinking age of the country you reside in and be aware of the drinking age in any country you visit in case they differ.

Alcohol is the content in spirits, wine, and beer that causes the intoxicating effects when they are drunk. Alcohol causes health issues such as liver disease and cancer when consumed in high amounts for long periods of time. It is especially damaging to teens due to their developmental stage.

Alcohol consumption in teens has physiological, psychological, emotional, and social impacts, including the following:

1) It can damage their growing brain and disrupt its normal growth.

2) It leads to poor decision-making.

3) It increases their risk-taking behaviour.

4) They are more likely to engage in sexual activities and regret it.

5) It enhances their emotions when drunk.

6) Teens who drink together encourage further drinking.

7) They have higher rates of accidents when drinking.

8) It increases antisocial behaviour.

9) It inhibits physical coordination.

10) It can cause alcohol poisoning.

11) It disrupts sleep.

12) It impacts school attendance and performance.

13) Alcohol is depressive and can increase feelings of anxiety.

14) Alcohol can increase aggression.

15) It can result in current and future addiction.

With all these issues associated with alcohol, why do teens still drink?

1) They don't really comprehend the impact alcohol has on them.

2) Teens are wired for risky behaviour and trying new things, including alcohol.

3) They feel peer pressure to drink alcohol and want to fit in.

4) To feel relaxed or less anxious about something.

5) For confidence, as alcohol lessens their inhibitions.

6) Drinking is role-modelled by adults in their lives.

7) They have mental health challenges and use it for self-medicating.

8) They use it to escape life situations, such as an abusive or unstable home environment.

9) As an act of defiance.

10) They are bored, and it's something to do.

11) The media portrays drinking as something that doesn't have consequences and normalises it.

12) Alcohol is addictive as it works on the reward circuit of the brain and releases the feel good hormone dopamine. This feeling doesn't last long, so teens will continue drinking in order to get that feeling back.

13) They have a genetic predisposition to addictive behaviours.

How do you know if your teen is drinking alcohol? In isolation, some of these may not mean they are drinking, but in combination, it can be a sign they are:

1) Their behaviour is out of character.
2) You notice alcohol disappearing from your personal supply at home.
3) They look intoxicated, or you smell alcohol on them.
4) They chew gum a lot and have mints or brush their teeth at strange times to disguise the smell on their breath.
5) They are sneaking around and being secretive. For example, not allowing you in their room or near their bags.
6) They're going out more and/or to new places.
7) They ask for money or spend money with nothing to show for it.
8) You are aware their friends drink because it increases the likelihood they are.
9) They have recently changed their friendship group and might drink to fit in with them.
10) They are moody or irritable.
11) Their school performance drops.
12) They get sick more than usual, particularly after going out with friends.

The big question is, should you allow your teen to drink small amounts of alcohol when they're underage? I was raised in the era where it was the norm for parents to give their older teens alcohol in moderation, with the opinion it would prevent them from drinking excessively and teach them responsible drinking habits. Furthermore, their teens would be drinking under their supervision, which they believed was better than hiding their drinking and consuming alcohol in unsafe situations. Officials even said it was okay. However, a study called Growing Up in Australia, the Longitudinal Study of Australian Children (LSAC) carried out in 2016, has caused experts to revise their recommendations.

The study surveyed the drinking habits of 3,000 teenagers and their families in Australia, where the legal age of drinking is 18, with some interesting results. The key findings were:

1) More than a quarter of 16 and 17-year-olds were allowed to drink alcohol at home.
2) 18 % of teens aged 16 and 17 were allowed to take alcohol to parties.
3) Alcohol use was significantly higher among those teens aged 16 to 17 who were allowed to drink at home compared to their peers who were not.
4) Teens whose families permitted them to drink at home had a higher likelihood of experiencing alcohol-related harm than those without permission, such as trouble at school or work the day following drinking, violence or fights at school, alcohol-related injuries, or engaging in sexual activities when drinking and later regretting it.

So what do you do if your teen is drinking, and how do you help them stop?

1) Don't freak out. Collect yourself and make a plan of action.
2) Reflect on your own use of alcohol and what you are role modelling.
3) Speak to your teen about your concerns at an appropriate time for you both, such as when you are calm and have no time restrictions or distractions. Be curious and non-judgemental.
4) Ask your teen why they drink.
5) Ask your teen if they know the impacts of alcohol.
6) Have them reflect on how they genuinely feel when they drink and afterward. Do they really enjoy it?

7) Educate them on the risks of alcohol.

8) Help them improve their feelings literacy and emotional regulation so they don't drink when they have uncomfortable feelings (chapter 6).

9) Improve their self-esteem (chapter 5) and self-respect as they will be less likely to drink.

10) Work on their communication skills so they can express what's troubling them instead of drinking (chapter 8).

11) Assist them in building boundaries if they feel that it's peer pressure and help them assertively express these boundaries.

12) If your teen feels uncomfortable at a party or another situation where there is alcohol, you can use a code word or emoji that your teen texts you. You respond by calling them and telling them there is a family emergency and you need to collect them immediately. This gives your teen a way out of any situation they are uncomfortable in or feel at risk in. It's important you tell your teen that they don't need to explain themselves if they don't want to, so they feel confident to use it.

13) Talk about their values and goals. See if drinking alcohol aligns with them.

14) Encourage your teen to take up a physical activity or sport, as they are less likely to drink.

15) Suggest they get a new hobby or interest to focus on.

16) What could they save money for and buy instead of alcohol?

17) Encourage them to reflect on their friendships. Maybe find new ones who don't drink?

18) Address any mental health concerns with a mental health professional.

As a parent, you should encourage your teen to delay drinking as late as possible to reduce their risk of harm and employ the protective factors against addiction made earlier in this chapter.

Drugs

Teens may use prescription or illegal drugs for recreational purposes. Excluding alcohol and nicotine, the most common drugs currently used by teens are marijuana, prescription drugs, inhalants, and spice.

Below is a summary of the drugs teens may use or be exposed to and the general effects they have on a person's body. Remember, teens will be more vulnerable to these side effects and long-term damage due to their underdeveloped brains and still-maturing bodies. Teens are also less capable of managing the emotional effects of drugs and their social consequences. Furthermore, as drugs lower inhibitions, teens may put themselves at further risk than they are already susceptible to doing. The effects of drugs are exacerbated when they are mixed or used with alcohol.

Marijuana or Cannabis

Cannabis is the general name for drugs made from the cannabis sativa plant, and the active ingredient is Tetrahydrocannabinol (THC). Marijuana is the most common form and is made from the dried leaves and flowers of the plant (it looks like a bud or herbs). It is smoked either as a joint, like a hand-rolled cigarette, or in a bong, and the vapour is inhaled. Other forms of cannabis are hashish (a solid form), hash oil (you dip the tip of the joint or the cigarette into it), and concentrate (cannabis extract dissolved in oil). Cannabis has medical uses and is legal in some states and countries.

Cannabis is easy for teens to get, making it extremely popular, and some teens don't even believe it's a real drug. It is often thought to be a gateway drug to using other substances, but there is actually little evidence supporting this. Furthermore, most teens are not defined as regular users and serious harm is rare. However, it's wise to be aware of the effects and impacts smoking cannabis can have on your teen physiologically, psychologically, and socially.

So, what does marijuana do to your teen?

1) It causes spontaneous laughter.
2) They may feel calm and content.
3) They may feel anxious or paranoid.
4) It slows their reflexes.
5) It is usually smoked with friends, so it is sociable.
6) It inhibits memory.
7) It causes dry mouth.
8) It increases appetite, called "the munchies."
9) It results in red, bloodshot eyes.
10) It impedes balance.
11) It increases heart rate.
12) It can cause nausea and vomiting.
13) It may make them tired and sleepy.

Long-term and regular cannabis use has further effects:

1) It stops them from doing other things because of the time and energy spent on smoking.
2) As cannabis is smoked and usually mixed with tobacco in joints, there are also similar risks associated with cigarettes on a teen's health.
3) It reduces school performance as it impacts their memory and learning.
4) It reduces their ability to restrain their behaviour.
5) In some cases, it leads to cannabis use disorder, which is an addiction to the substance.
6) They can experience cannabis withdrawal when they stop using it abruptly.
7) They have twice the chance of developing schizophrenia.
8) It can impact menstruation and make periods irregular.
9) It can reduce spasm count.

10) It can lower sex drive.

Painkillers and Prescription Drugs

Prescription drugs are relatively easy for teens to obtain compared to street drugs, as they may have access to their parents' prescription medications, can get them through friends, or buy them. However, it is illegal to use a drug for something it has not been prescribed for, and it can be very dangerous. The most commonly abused prescription drugs can be categorised as opioids, central nervous system (CNS) depressants, and stimulants.

- *Opioids:*

  Opioids are mainly used to relieve moderate to severe pain. They prevent the brain from receiving pain messages by attaching to the opioid receptors or nerve cells in the central nervous system (the brain and spinal cord), gut, and other areas of the body. They block pain signals sent from the body via the spinal cord to the brain.

  Side effects of recreational use can include euphoria, nausea and vomiting, constipation, physical dependence, confusion, headaches, dizziness, difficulty breathing, and it can impede thinking.

  Examples of opioids you may have heard of are OxyContin, Vicodin, and Demerol.

- *CNS Depressants:*

  These are used to treat anxiety, panic attacks, tension, and sleep disorders as they cause a calming or drowsy effect. CNS depressants do this by increasing the activity of GABA, a neurotransmitter in the brain that slows down brain activity. Teens using CNS depressants for recreational purposes may also experience confusion, impaired concentration, lower blood pressure, slowed breathing, mood swings, vivid dreams, and nightmares. It may lead to seizures if stopped abruptly.

Examples of CNS depression you may have heard of are Valium and Xanax.

- *Stimulants:*

This group of prescription drugs increase activity in the central nervous system by interacting with different neurotransmitter systems, such as norephedrine and dopamine. Stimulants are mostly used to treat attention-deficit hyperactivity disorder (ADHD) and narcolepsy, as they increase energy levels, alertness, and focus attention. As stimulants are used for ADHD, it makes them accessible to teens. When used by someone who doesn't have ADHD, however, these drugs may cause seizures or heart failure. They can raise body temperature dangerously high, cause headaches and irregular heartbeat, aggression, paranoia, psychosis, nerve and stomach issues.

Examples of stimulants you may have heard of are Ritalin and Adderall.

Inhalants and Huffing

Inhalants are volatile substances whose fumes or vapour are inhaled for their psychedelic (mind-altering) effects. These include household products such as glue, cleaning products, shoe cleaner, hairspray, and oil sprays, and other products such as paint spray, markers, propane tanks, and lighter fluid. They are cheap, legal, and easy to access for teens. They provide an immediate high. However, as the effects are very short-lived, users will often inhale the substance repeatedly to prolong them. Doing so over a long period of time can have an aesthetic impact, producing a numbing feeling and can result in the user losing consciousness.

Huffing (the misuse of inhalants) is extremely dangerous and can result in sudden sniffing death. When high concentrations of these chemicals are inhaled, they can cause oxygen to be displaced from the lungs, resulting in a loss of consciousness and suffocation or they can directly cause a heart attack.

Other side effects of huffing are:

1) Hallucinations.
2) Headaches.
3) Dizziness.
4) Slurred speech.
5) Disorientation.
6) Irritability.
7) Impeded coordination.
8) Rashes around the nose and damage to the nasal passages.
9) Euphoria.
10) Loss of appetite.
11) Limb spasms and muscle cramps.
12) Hearing loss.
13) Memory loss.
14) Convulsions.
15) Seizures.
16) Kidney or liver damage.
17) Coma.
18) Damage to the brain and nervous system.
19) Damage to bone marrow.

Spice or K2

Synthetic cannabis is made by adding chemicals to herbs. They're designed to mimic the side effects of THC in cannabis and are more harmful and unpredictable than cannabis due to their chemicals. They smell like cannabis and are also smoked.

Other Drugs

Cocaine

The active ingredient in cocaine is extracted from the leaves of the cocoa plant, processed, and blended with other chemicals into a white powder. It is a stimulant drug that works on the central nervous system and speeds up the messaging between the brain and the rest of the body. It produces a euphoric feeling by increasing levels of dopamine in the brain.

Cocaine is usually snorted, which can result in nose bleeds and a loss of smell, but it can also be mixed with water and injected. Cocaine can make a person more talkative and increase their energy levels. It also impacts sleep, increases the heart rate, causes muscle spasms, and can result in convulsions. It can cause feelings of paranoia, anxiety, and anger. Cocaine can impact decision-making and impulse control, which is already compromised in teens. It is addictive and can result in seizures, heart attacks, strokes, and coma. Luckily, cocaine is not used by many teens as it can be fatal.

Hallucinogens, LSD, PCP, Ketamine, and Magic Mushrooms

Hallucinogens can be ingested in pill, capsule, or liquid form and affect areas of the brain associated with sensory input, distorting a person's perception of reality. Individuals may see, smell, hear, or touch things that aren't actually there. Some hallucinogens are synthetic, such as LSD, PCP, and Ketamine, while others, like Magic Mushrooms, are found naturally in certain plants.

These drugs can have varying onset times and effects, depending on factors such as an individual's height and weight, their mood when taking the drug, general health, past experiences with the drug, the environment they're in, and their company. Interactions with other drugs can also influence their impact. Hallucinogens can sometimes cause synesthesia, where senses cross over; for example, a person might "see" sounds.

Effects might include a distortion of space and time, feelings of relaxation, or sensations of being separated from one's body.

Physical side effects can encompass dilated pupils, an increased heart rate, appetite suppression, and nausea. Other potential side effects include muscle spasms, a loss of concentration, convulsions, aggressive and violent behaviour, and catatonic syndrome. Hallucinogens can impair judgement, leading to risky and dangerous behaviour. There's also the risk of experiencing a "bad trip," where the hallucinations become frightening, leading to paranoia and intense panic. Some users may experience flashbacks even when not under the influence, and drugs like Ketamine and PCP can lead to withdrawals, as they can be addictive. Synthetic drugs pose an added risk because it's often impossible to know exactly what they contain.

DXM

Dextromethorphan (DXM) is an ingredient in over-the-counter cough and cold medications. Used in high doses, it can have similar effects as PCP and Ketamine. It can cause hallucinations and dissociation. Other effects include a rash, sweating, lethargy or hyperactivity, hot flushes, impaired judgement and coordination, high blood pressure and a racing heart, slurred speech, nausea and vomiting, dizziness, and paranoia. It is good to be aware of this if you keep cough and cold medications at home, which your teen could access.

MDMA, Ecstasy, or Molly

MDMA is a stimulant, psychedelic, and empathogen (it increases feelings of compassion and empathy). It is commonly ingested either in pill or tablet form or snorted as a powder, but it can also be smoked and injected. It is popular among teens who like to party as it's specifically designed to cause a high and increase energy levels. The effects last for around 3 to 4 hours. Users can experience a 'come down' after taking the drug, which can last up to two days. MDMA can be mixed with other chemicals, which may be dangerous and result in unexpected side effects. MDMA can cause feelings of euphoria, increased confidence and libido, and a loss of inhibition. Physical symptoms include dilated pupils, sweating, dehydration and excessive thirst, an accelerated heart rate and breathing, a rise in blood pressure, jaw clenching and teeth grinding, loss of appetite, sleep problems, and nausea. MDMA has the potential to cause liver, kidney, and heart damage, muscle breakdown, brain swelling, brain damage, and even death.

Heroin

Heroin is an opioid made from morphine and works by interacting with the opioid receptors in the brain, which are involved in pain control and transmission. As such, heroin reduces pain and elicits feelings of pleasure and relaxation. It comes in a powder, small granules, or in rock form. It is usually injected but can be smoked or snorted. Effects last between three to five hours and include feelings of drowsiness, clumsiness, confusion and detachment, slurred and slowed speech, dry mouth, tiny pupils, slowed breathing and heart rate, reduced appetite and sex drive, nausea, and death.

Heroin is addictive, cheap, and easier to obtain than other drugs. Although it is uncommon for teens to use, it is on the increase among young adults, so it is worth being aware of as a parent of a teen.

Ice and Meth

Ice, crystal meth, and meth are the same thing. However, crystal meth is in a purer form and thus more potent. It causes the brain to release more dopamine, so it elicits feelings of euphoria and increases energy levels. Its effects can last up to 24 hours, and it is extremely addictive. Ice, or crystal meth, looks like a rock or glass, while meth (speed or crank) looks like a fine powder or a brownish-yellow oil substance (base).

These drugs are injected or snorted depending on their form and may be mixed with many other substances. Meth can cause anxiety, depression, delusions, paranoia, aggression, violence, psychosis, overheating, strokes, and heart attacks. Long-term use can result in serious psychological disorders, tooth damage, skin sores, and extreme weight loss. Users experience a "crash" after the dopamine rush causes the brain's natural stores to deplete, leading to an addictive cycle. It can cause death.

With all these dangerous side effects, why do teens take drugs?

Teens take drugs for similar reasons that they drink alcohol or engage in other addictive behaviours:

1) They are developmentally more inclined to try new things and engage in risky behaviour.
2) They feel peer pressure from their friends.
3) They have mental health challenges, so use it to self-medicate.
4) As an escape or distraction from life.
5) Because of low self-esteem.
6) They have poor emotional regulation.
7) They are or feel socially isolated.
8) The adults in their lives role model and normalise drug taking.
9) They have limited or no boundaries and rules.
10) There is a lack of parental supervision.

11) They have access to the drugs.

12) They don't really understand the impacts drugs have on them.

How do you know if your teen is taking drugs? Drugs have different physical side effects (mentioned above), so it is good to be aware of them in case you identify them in your teen. However, there are some common signs your teen may be taking drugs:

1) They are secretive and act suspiciously. They may not let you in the room or near their belongings.

2) You notice changes in their behaviour.

3) They act defensively when you talk to them about their behaviour or drugs.

4) They smell differently.

5) You find drug paraphernalia, such as cigarette papers used for rolling joints.

6) You find strange-looking objects such as small colourful stamps, which could be LSD or a brown lump which may be hash.

7) Your prescription meds aren't lasting as long as they should, so you might be missing some.

8) They are sick more than usual.

9) They are regularly ill after going out with friends.

10) There are changes in their mood and/or they experience mood swings.

11) You're aware their friends are taking drugs.

12) Their school performance is worsening.

13) They don't want to go to school.

14) They're spending their money but have nothing to show for it.

15) They're going to new places.

16) They're out more or later at night.

17) There are changes in their weight.

18) You notice changes in their appetite or inconsistency in their appetite.

19) They are hanging out with new friends.

There is no denying it will be a scary and confronting time if you discover your teen is taking drugs, but there are things you can do:

1) Take time to process the information and respond; do not react.
2) Don't issue ultimatums or punish them, as this will push them further away and will not address the problem.
3) Pick an appropriate time to have a conversation about your concerns with your teen. Don't just accuse them, but state what you think, have been told, or found out. Be curious and ask them why they started taking the drugs and gather more information about the situation.
4) If they deny using any drugs, you can search their space. It is up to you whether you tell them beforehand, but be prepared for the pushback. Stick by your decision and your right to search their space because it is your job to keep them safe.
5) Ask your teen what they know about the drug, its effects, and the dangers. Educate them on what you know and suggest you research more about it together.
6) Raise the immediate impacts of drug use rather than long-term effects, as teens don't have the same capacity to think or care about long-term consequences. For example, they won't be able to perform well at sport on the weekend, or they will be "coming down" the day after taking drugs and feel too terrible to go out.
7) Help your teen improve their soft skills such as feelings literacy, emotional regulation (Chapter 6), resiliency (Chapter 7), and constructive communication (Chapter 8) so they don't turn to drugs when they feel challenged or out of control.
8) Encourage them to engage in more physical activities.
9) Suggest they find a hobby or other activities to focus on and get enjoyment from.
10) Help them build their self-esteem, as they will be less likely to disrespect themselves by taking drugs.

11) Help them identify their values and ask whether taking drugs aligns with them.

12) Help them plan or even role-play what to do in the future if they are offered drugs or in a situation where their friends and peers are taking them.

13) Your teen can send you a code when they wish to leave a situation. You call them, telling them it's a family emergency and you are collecting them immediately. It's important your teen knows they don't need to explain what happened if they don't want to, so they feel confident to use the code whenever they are in trouble or feel at risk.

14) Plan what your teen should do if they take drugs or are with anyone who has, and things go wrong. Explain they will never be in trouble for calling you.

15) Keep ongoing communication with your teen about drugs and how they are in general.

16) Address the underlying issues as to why your teen takes drugs.

17) Engage a mental health and/or addiction specialist.

18) Get support for yourself. It can be extremely frightening to discover your teen is taking drugs, and you may feel a sense of responsibility, which you should process.

Food Addiction

Food addiction is becoming increasingly more of an issue among adolescents. Research has shown junk food, processed food, and food too high in salt, fat, and sugar have addictive properties and stimulate the reward pathways of the brain, similar to drugs and alcohol, resulting in feel-good chemicals such as dopamine being released. This can lead to teens craving unhealthy foods and overeating them, as well as experiencing withdrawals when they are cut out of their diet because of their addictive properties. Food addiction is extremely problematic as it can lead to obesity and other health and life problems. The big difficulty with food addiction is that junk and processed food are readily available and often cheaper in comparison to healthier food products.

There are many reasons your teen may develop food addiction, including:

1) They have hormonal imbalances resulting in cravings.
2) The side effects of some medications cause cravings.
3) They have a genetic predisposition to addictive behaviours.
4) They use food to lift negative feelings, manage challenging situations, and avoid dealing with problems.
5) They've experienced abuse, neglect, or trauma.
6) They have an unstable home environment.
7) They feel peer pressure to eat certain foods.
8) They are socially isolated.
9) They have co-occurring mental health disorders and/or addictions.
10) They have been role-modelled unhealthy dietary habits by adults in their lives.

Food addiction can have serious impacts on your teen:

1) They can become overweight or obese.
2) It can lead to digestive issues.
3) It can cause acne and other skin conditions.
4) There's an increased risk of heart disease.
5) Diets high in calories, fat, and cholesterol increase the risk of type 2 diabetes.
6) It can cause chronic fatigue.
7) It can result in sleep disturbances.
8) It can cause headaches.
9) They may become malnourished.
10) It can lead to low self-esteem.
11) It can lead to feelings of guilt and shame.

12) It can cause depression.

13) It can result in anxiety.

14) They may have difficulty focusing.

How do you recognize if your teen has a food addiction?

1) They experience the health issues listed above.

2) They are irritable, especially if they cannot access particular foods.

3) They have decreased academic performance.

4) They are isolating themselves from family and friends.

5) They avoid social situations.

6) They're craving certain foods.

7) They're going out of their way to get particular food items.

8) They're eating to the point of feeling sick.

9) They're eating secretly.

10) They are restless.

11) They overeat, continuing to eat even when they're full.

12) Changes in their weight.

13) They set rules about bettering their eating habits but abide by them.

14) They are unable to quit eating certain foods despite the health implications.

There are a number of ways you can address food addiction in your teen and help them overcome it:

1) Be honest about your own diet, food habits, and those you instil in your household.

2) Speak to your teen about your concerns regarding their eating habits.

3) Ask them about their understanding of processed food, junk food, and their impact on their health.

4) Ask if there is anything going on in their life causing them stress or concern.

5) Don't completely cut out the foods they enjoy, but work towards them having a balanced diet of "everyday food and sometimes food."

6) Talk to a nutritionist and make a healthy eating plan with your teen.

7) Make dietary changes slowly so the new habits stick.

8) Teach your teen to cook and prepare their own healthy meals.

9) Suggest your teen engage in more physical activity or start a sport, one they feel comfortable doing.

10) Get on board as a family and improve your diet and exercise habits together.

11) Be prepared for your teen to experience withdrawals from the foods they are addicted to and prepare them for withdrawal symptoms.

12) Help them find other healthy ways to replace the feel-good hormones they get through food.

13) Engage the support of a therapist to address the addiction and any other underlying issues.

Compulsive Exercise

It is also possible for your teen to develop an addiction to exercise because of its ability to produce adrenaline, dopamine, endorphins, and other feel-good hormones. Teens usually start off in a genuine attempt to be healthy or lose weight, but it becomes excessive. Teenage athletes are also vulnerable to exercise addiction due to their drive to be better and achieve more in their chosen sport. Exercise addiction occurs in a relatively small number of teens, with the largest representation being seen in adolescents with eating disorders. Over-exercise in this context is usually a result of teens wanting to have the ideal and often an attainable body portrayed by the media (I'll discuss this in detail in Chapter 5).

There are a range of factors that can cause a teen to develop exercise addiction:

1) Genetic predisposition to addictive behaviours.

2) Exercise releases feel-good hormones associated with the reward circuit of the brain.

3) They use exercise as a distraction.

4) They have a negative body image.

5) They have low self-esteem.

6) They have an eating disorder.

7) They feel peer pressure to engage in overexercising and/or there are group norms around excessive exercise, such as in sport.

8) They have been or are being bullied for their physical appearance.

The difficulty with exercise and physical activity is that it's socially desirable and a positive aspect of a healthy lifestyle, meaning it can become a serious problem before the issue is identified. So, how can you tell if your teen is becoming compulsive about exercise?

1) They can't miss an exercise session.

2) They abide by a strict exercise schedule.

3) They exercise multiple times a day.

4) Their workouts are longer than a 'normal' session.

5) They get irritable or panicked when they can't exercise or if they cut a session short.

6) They exercise at strange or inappropriate times.

7) They hide the amount of exercise they do.

8) They are constantly thinking and talking about exercise.

9) Exercise is more important to them than seeing family and friends.

10) Exercise interferes with other life activities.

11) They never feel satisfied with how long or hard they exercise or with their physical achievements.

12) Their self-esteem is tied to their physical achievements and the amount of exercise they do.

13) They never miss a workout session, even if they are ill, injured or tired.

14) They are losing their enjoyment of exercise.

15) You notice changes in their appetite.

16) They experience injuries and prolonged muscle soreness.

17) Irregular periods or amenorrhea (absence of a period) in girls.

18) They have chronic fatigue

19) They have a low resting heart rate.

What should you do if you think your teen is addicted to exercise?

1) Raise your concerns with your teen and say why you have them.

2) Discuss how exercise can be addictive and the harmful effects of compulsive exercise.

3) Ask why they feel the need to exercise the way they do.

4) Collaborate on an exercise plan that includes shorter sessions, a reduced number of sessions, high and low-intensity exercises, and rest days.

5) Be conscious of any injuries they may have or develop and treat them.

6) Talk to their coach/physical education teacher/trainer about your concerns (if applicable).

7) Encourage them to find other ways to reduce their stress.

8) Help them improve their soft skills, such as emotional regulation and constructive communication, so they can manage difficult emotions and express them rather than using exercise to deal with them.

9) Find fun ways to exercise and keep active with your teen or as a family.

10) Help them make nutritious meals that meet the requirements of their active body.

11) Engage professional support for your teen.

12) Get support for yourself, either from a friend or professional.

Conclusion

While teens are developmentally prone to addiction for many reasons, not all of them fall into this trap. Many experiment with drugs and/or alcohol or carry out activities like gaming without forming an addiction. Understanding the mechanics of addiction and recognizing what makes a teen vulnerable allows you to implement protective measures. These measures can either prevent addiction from forming or allow you to respond promptly when signs of addiction appear. The central question regarding addiction is: why did your teen partake in a particular substance or activity to such an extent that they became addicted?

The decision a teen makes to choose one substance or activity over another can be influenced by numerous factors. For instance, their values around drugs and alcohol might mean they avoid these substances and instead turn to exercise. They might have easy access to processed and fast food, leading to bingeing and potential addiction. Alternatively, if their parents drink alcohol excessively, this might normalise and encourage drinking behaviours.

I understand the impulse to panic or get angry if your teen continues to act destructively. However, reacting strongly can push them further into their addiction. It's crucial to understand the "why" behind their actions before addressing "what" they are doing. The reasons can range from bullying, low self-esteem, and academic struggles to seeking an escape from life's challenges. It's essential to guide your teen towards healthier coping strategies. If not, they'll carry these harmful coping mechanisms into adulthood, relying on them in challenging times.

The deeper these habits are ingrained, the harder they are to change. If you suspect your teen is developing an addiction, whether to substances like alcohol or drugs or behaviours like excessive eating, exercise, gaming, or social media use, seeking professional assistance is vital. Withdrawal symptoms can arise from curtailing or stopping these activities. Moreover, addressing the root causes of the addictive behaviour is crucial. Otherwise, they're likely to relapse or simply swap one addiction for another.

CHAPTER 5

The Mind-Field of Adolescence

"Help your teen focus on the good things in life no matter how small or insignificant they may seem, it will literally wire their brain for happiness."

I have an understanding of mental health through my psychology degree, trauma-informed training, and my work with young people. I even have lived experience of it. However, I am not a mental health specialist, so if you are concerned in any way for your teen's mental health, please seek out professional help.

Someone's mental health refers to their collective emotional, psychological, and social well-being. If a teen is struggling with their mental health or has a mental health illness, their thoughts, feelings, and behaviours will be affected, as will their ability to handle stress, make decisions, interact with, and relate to others.

Multiple factors impact a teen's mental health, making them vulnerable to mental health illnesses and increasing the likelihood of them engaging in risk-taking behaviours such as drinking and drug misuse. Therefore, understanding factors that may contribute to a teen developing a mental health disorder can both assist you in supporting your teen psychologically and address any addictive behaviours they may have. In this chapter, I will discuss the most common mental health illnesses experienced by teenagers.

Self-Esteem

Self-esteem is how your teen sees and values themselves and their abilities. Their level of self-esteem is impacted by a complex interaction of factors, and in turn, influences different aspects of their life, such as their mental health and body image. Although low self-esteem can have detrimental effects on your teen, having healthy self-esteem provides a huge protective factor against the challenges of adolescence.

Types of Self-Esteem

Unhealthy

- *Low self-esteem.*

  People with low self-esteem do not value themselves or believe in themselves or in their abilities. They are insecure, and their fear of failure prevents them from acting on things. They are sensitive people who are easily influenced and do not readily defend their opinions.

- *Inflated sense of self.*

  It may surprise you, but a person can have too much self-esteem. Those with inflated levels of self-esteem think they are better than everyone else. They are extremely competitive, cannot critique themselves, are unable to listen to other people's points of view and opinions, and don't accept fault. They have difficulty forming and maintaining healthy relationships.

Healthy

- *High self-esteem.*

  People with high self-esteem recognize and acknowledge both their strengths and areas of growth, so their view of themselves is balanced and accurate. They take feedback well and do not attach their sense of worth to others' opinions of them.

There are numerous factors influencing a teen's level of self-esteem:

1) A number of studies have shown genetics contributes to self-esteem.
2) Girls and women generally have lower self-esteem than boys and men.
3) Some personalities are predisposed to having higher levels of self-esteem, such as extroverts and conscientious individuals, while others are more likely to have lower self-esteem, such as introverts and empaths.
4) Negative and self-critical thoughts can reduce levels of self-esteem.
5) Better physical health is usually associated with healthier self-esteem
6) Teens with mental health challenges often lack self-esteem.
7) A teen is more likely to have healthy self-esteem if their home environment is nurturing and their parents appreciate and encourage their strengths.
8) Teens with adults in their lives who role model healthy self-esteem are more likely to have higher levels of self-esteem themselves. And those who see adults exhibiting behaviours associated with low levels of self-esteem are also likely to have lower self-esteem.
9) Those with greater levels of achievement usually have higher self-esteem, though this can develop into an inflated sense of self.
10) Depending on their proficiency in particular tasks, a teen's self-esteem may be negatively or positively impacted.

11) Teens who compare themselves to others often have lower levels of self-esteem.

12) Those who receive feedback negatively have lower levels of self-esteem, while those who accept feedback and use it to improve have healthy self-esteem.

13) Teens who seek extrinsic validation have lower levels of self-esteem than those who practise internal validation.

Teenagers with high self-esteem will exhibit some or all of the following traits:

1) They communicate their feelings and needs assertively.
2) They act assertively without guilt.
3) They know their value.
4) They appreciate themselves.
5) They focus on the present and don't dwell on the past.
6) They know they are equal to everyone else, not better or worse than anyone.
7) They don't take criticism personally and use it to grow.
8) They accept challenges and take risks.
9) They form loving and respectful relationships and maintain them.
10) They do not attach their sense of worth to other people's opinions of them.
11) They know failure leads to growth and learning.
12) They have healthy boundaries and express them.
13) They have self-respect and take care of themselves.
14) They have healthy levels of self-confidence.
15) They are motivated.
16) They set achievable goals and work towards them.

The good news is that self-esteem can be built. So, how can you help your teen develop a healthy level of self-esteem? Try some of these:

1) Help them to have realistic expectations of themselves so they are not constantly falling short of them, which will chip away at their self-esteem.

2) Have them set achievable goals, then break them down into smaller goals that they can easily attain. This enables them to see progress towards their goal and have a sense of accomplishment.

3) Encourage them to stop comparing themselves to others and focus on themselves.

4) Talk to them about their friendships. It is commonly said we are the sum of the five people we spend most time with, so what are your teen's friends like? Do they have low or high self-esteem? How do they treat or talk to your teen? Are your teens' friends contributing to their low self-esteem? If so, suggest they meet new friends who support and nourish them.

5) Suggest they take on a hobby or activity or learn something new that is within their skillset so they can start to build proficiency in something.

6) Make sure they acknowledge their effort and achievements.

7) Have them take a self-esteem inventory of ten strengths and ten areas of growth, as this gives a realistic conception of the self.

8) Help them stop being a perfectionist, and don't expect them to be perfect.

9) Help them reframe failure as a learning opportunity.

10) Encourage them to regularly write down one or two things they appreciate about themselves.

11) Challenge the way they talk to themselves both internally and out loud. Have them speak to themselves as they would a close friend. They could write a text to their best friend containing their internal

dialogue, then ask themselves, *Would I send this to my friend?* The answer is likely a resounding "NO!"

12) Help them build resiliency so they don't take things personally or let setbacks diminish their self-esteem (Chapter 7).

13) Assist them in learning constructive communication so they can confidently and assertively communicate their opinions, feelings, and needs (Chapter 8).

14) Help them increase their emotional intelligence (Chapter 6)

15) Be honest about your own level of self-esteem and the behaviours you exhibit in front of your teen.

16) Role model what healthy self-esteem looks like.

17) Find someone your teen admires who can coach or mentor them.

18) Suggest they engage in therapy if their low self-esteem is seriously impacting other areas of their life.

Depression and Anxiety

Globally, depression is one of the leading causes of illnesses and disability among adolescents, and suicide is the fourth leading cause of death in 15 to 19-year-olds worldwide (World Health Organization, 2020). Anxiety and depression are the most common psychological disorders among children and adolescents (Unicef, 2019). Statistics like these are frightening and certainly do not stand in isolation. The impact of COVID-19 on teens has only exacerbated the issue of mental health.

Teens with depression are characterised by a persistent low mood and experience a loss of interest in normal activities and the things they used to enjoy. It can severely impact their day-to-day life. Anxiety is when a teen has excessive and persistent worries and fears about daily events. These emotions are accompanied by physical symptoms such as an increased heart rate.

From here on in, I will also refer to anxiety and depression collectively as "mental health" for ease. However, I acknowledge there are many other mental health illnesses and disorders usually grouped under the umbrella of "mental health" I will not be addressing.

So, how do you know if your teen is just being a teen or if there's more to be concerned about? There are a number of factors, such as the following, that may make your teen more vulnerable to mental health struggles. However, particularly in isolation, they do not guarantee your teen will develop a mental health issue because mental health is the result of a complex interaction of factors.

1) They are in the early stages of puberty, experiencing a lot of physiological, mental, emotional, and social changes.
2) They are experiencing elements of puberty as an outlier. For example, they're very tall, have large breasts, start menstruation early, or have bad acne.
3) They are struggling with the workload at school.
4) They are feeling pressured to get or maintain excellent grades, excel at sport, music, or other extracurricular activities.
5) They are having issues with their friendship group.
6) They are being bullied at school, outside of it, or online.
7) They are socially isolated.
8) There are past or current disruptions to the family unit and home life.
9) They have experienced loss, for example, a break up of friendships or romantic relationships, death of a loved one.
10) They are facing or have experienced big life changes such as moving house or school.
11) They often express concern about the future.
12) They need to be in control.
13) They attach their self-worth to their appearance and/or achievements.

14) There is a family history of mental health.

15) They have experienced trauma, abuse and/or neglect.

Here are some signs your teen might be facing mental health challenges:

1) Their school performance has decreased.

2) Their achievements at extracurricular activities, such as sport or music, have declined.

3) They are withdrawing from loved ones, friends, and family members.

4) There is a change in their character, "they're just not themselves."

5) They are losing interest in the things they used to enjoy. They have a "don't care attitude."

6) They have stopped looking after their appearance and personal hygiene.

7) You notice a reduced or increased appetite, disordered or restricted eating habits.

8) There is a noticeable change in their weight.

9) Their sleep patterns are disturbed. They are sleeping a lot and/or fatigued or have insomnia.

10) They express feelings of sadness or low mood.

11) Their moods are erratic and extreme.

12) They tell you they are having problems and struggling.

13) They are drinking alcohol and/or taking drugs and engaging in other problematic risk-taking behaviours.

14) They are being extremely defiant and argumentative.

15) They are self-harming. This can involve cutting, burning, scratching or biting the skin, pulling hair, hitting themself, or putting themselves in dangerous situations.

It is extremely scary to discover your teen may be experiencing a mental health illness. So what can you do to support them and keep them safe?

1) Take time to process your feelings around the possibility your teen is experiencing a mental health challenge before approaching your teen about it.

2) Ask your teen questions that require a more detailed response. Instead of asking, "How was school?"—to which they'll likely respond with a simple "Fine"—pose open-ended questions that necessitate a longer answer. For instance, "What was your favourite part of the day and why?" or "What was the most challenging part of your day and why?" By doing so, you'll gain a better understanding of their experiences and encourage them to open up.

3) Choose an appropriate time for a conversation about their current struggles and how you can best support them. Be curious and non-judgemental. Don't accuse them, but say that you're concerned about them and believe they may have, for example, depression.

4) If you believe it is appropriate, encourage them to research mental health as they may not realise that's what they are experiencing.

5) Discuss using an app with your teen that monitors specific websites and internet content on their phone and alerts you to any concerning activity, for example, that may suggest signs of anxiety or depression in your teen. Explain this is for their safety and not an infringement on their privacy.

6) Help them adopt healthier eating habits, engage in some physical activity, and improve their sleep hygiene.

7) Explain that alcohol and drugs will only make things worse, even if they feel it helps at the time.

8) Reduce any stress for them that you can, for example, address bullying, limit extracurricular activities, or give them fewer chores at home.

9) Help your teen increase their emotional literacy and emotional regulation so they can identify and process their feelings (Chapter 6).

10) Help them improve other soft skills, such as constructive communication (Chapter 8) and resilience (Chapter 7).

11) If your teen won't speak with you, encourage them to find a safe adult they can talk to, such as a family friend or friend's parent.

12) Suggest they start a gratitude journal to help them focus on the positive things in their life. Saying positive affirmations and making vision boards displaying things that make them happy and/or they would like to achieve can also help your teen shift their mindset.

13) Have your teen name up to five safe adults you can talk to about their struggles to help keep them safe. Discuss with your teen how much information they are comfortable with you sharing.

14) For your teen's safety, consider talking to their school in confidence.

15) Openly discuss what mental health is and how there is no shame around it. Many people experience mental health challenges in their lifetime. The World Health Organization reported in 2019 that one in eight people (970 million people) were living with a mental health disorder. This rose in 2020 due to the impacts of COVID by 26 % for anxiety and 28 % for depression.

16) Suggest they research some famous people who have experienced anxiety or depression to reduce any stigma your teen may feel.

17) Do you know anyone who has experienced mental health who your teen could talk to?

18) Try not to sweat the small stuff, such as making them tidy their room, picking them up on their language, or worrying about their academic performance for the time being. They're emotionally and possibly physically unsafe, so this is the priority.

19) Work on increasing their self-esteem and self-worth.

20) Suggest they volunteer or do something else that gives them a sense of purpose.

21) Get professional guidance on what to do.

22) Have your teen assessed for mental health and addiction (if applicable). Inform them this is for their safety and do not do it behind their back as they need to trust you.

23) Suggest they join a support group of other teens experiencing mental health struggles. They will feel less isolated connecting with teens who have a shared experience.

24) Get support for yourself, as it will be a challenging and emotional time.

Self-Harm

When teens self-harm, they intentionally cause themselves physical injury or put themselves at risk. This can manifest as cutting, burning, hitting, or punching themselves. Other forms include abusing alcohol and other substances, engaging in unsafe sex, getting into physical fights, or exercising to the point of exhaustion or injury.

Teens might resort to self-harm as a way to transmute emotional pain into physical pain, trying to cope with, express, or control intense negative feelings, distressing memories, or overwhelming thoughts. While self-harm might offer momentary relief, the challenging emotions often return, potentially leading to a cyclical and compulsive pattern of self-harming behaviour.

Some signs your teen may be self-harming include:

1) Unexplained injuries or wounds they say are accidental.

2) They have unexplained scars.

3) They wear clothes with long sleeves and/or that cover their legs to hide their skin, even when it is not appropriate. For example, in hot weather.

4) They avoid situations where people may see their skin.

5) They keep sharp objects accessible to them.

6) You see them rubbing their skin or picking at it.

7) There is blood on their clothes, bedding, towels, or on tissues.

8) They openly talk about it.

Discovering your teen is self-harming can be extremely frightening, but there are things you can do to support your teen, specifically around the self-harming behaviours:

1) Compose yourself and try not to panic. Easier said than done, I know.

2) Reduce or eliminate, as best as possible, their access to harmful objects, such as knives, razor blades, scissors, and lighters.

3) Talk about their self-harm in a compassionate and non-judgemental way. Express your concerns and let them know it is upsetting and worrying for you to see them harm themselves, and you want to support them. See if your teen can verbalise why they self-harm and how it helps them so you can understand it.

4) Suggest they keep a diary and journal their feelings, thoughts, and experiences so they can try to identify triggers for self-harming. Why do they do it one time and not another?

5) Come up with a safety plan for your teen around their self-harming behaviours. For example, they give you a secret sign so you know they want to self-harm and can support them or simply keep them occupied. They might agree to do an activity they enjoy, such as listening to music, dancing, or exercising if they feel triggered. Something that expels the overwhelming thoughts and feelings. They could also use breathing and grounding exercises to bring them into the present and focus on the now.

6) Although there's limited evidence it works, they could use less harmful methods of self-harming, such as holding an ice cube or flicking an elastic band on their wrist.

7) If you haven't already, try to engage your teen with a mental health professional. Involve them in the process and keep looking until they find one they connect with. If they already have a therapist, encourage your teen to discuss their self-harming with them.

8) Get them immediate medical attention if the self-harm requires it.

Suicidal Ideation

Suicidal ideation is when a teen has thoughts of ending their own life and may have plans on how to do it. Many teens who have suicidal ideation or attempt suicide have mental health illnesses and struggle with the challenges of being a teen. They may feel helpless and hopeless about their life and can't see solutions to their problems, so they believe suicide is the only answer. Unfortunately, the risk of suicide increases significantly in adolescents. Boys die by suicide four times as often as girls, although girls think about and attempt suicide twice as much as boys. This is likely due to the more lethal and violent methods boys use compared to girls, such as firearms versus pharmaceutical drug overdoses.

Why a teen has suicidal ideation is extremely complex. However, there are factors that make a teen more vulnerable to suicide, especially if they are experiencing multiple factors concurrently or consecutively and have limited protective factors to mitigate them.

1) They self-harm.
2) They have a mental health illness.
3) There is a family history of mental health illness or suicide.
4) They know someone with suicidal thoughts and tendencies.
5) They have directly known a friend or family member who has committed suicide.
6) They abuse substances.
7) They struggle with the changes of puberty.

8) They have or are currently experiencing major life changes such as relocating, transferring schools, or parental separation.

9) They are experiencing a long-term illness.

10) They are in conflict with family members and/or friends.

11) The breakdown of important relationships

12) They are a victim of abuse or violence, either historically or currently, including bullying.

13) They are adopted.

14) They are gender diverse or struggling with their sexuality and are unsupported by their family or community. These teens are especially vulnerable when they experience another risk factor.

15) They have access to the means of committing suicide, for example, over-the-counter medication and firearms.

16) They have previously attempted suicide.

How do you know your teen is at risk of suicide? If taken in isolation, some of these may point to other issues discussed in this book, but if you identify a number of them in your teen, they may be experiencing suicidal ideation. Others are clear indicators your teen is at risk of significant harm to themselves:

1) Moodiness.

2) They withdraw and isolate themselves from loved ones.

3) They no longer enjoy or engage in things they used to do.

4) They talk about death and suicide or seem very interested in it.

5) They don't care about anything.

6) They've lost interest in school, and their academic performance has worsened.

7) They are no longer interested in extracurricular activities.

8) They express feelings of helplessness and hopelessness.

9) They give away belongings, especially important ones, for seemingly no reason.

10) They don't talk about or make plans for the future.

11) They write about loss, death, suicide, or separation in letters, poems, or songs.

12) They have trouble concentrating.

13) They have disrupted sleep, insomnia, or sleep a lot.

14) There are changes in their eating habits.

15) They engage in risky behaviour.

16) You notice medicines are missing.

17) They directly express thoughts of suicide.

18) They may appear suddenly happy or positive because they've decided to commit suicide, and it's a relief.

What should you do if you think your teenager is at risk of suicide? As well as referring to the prior suggestions under mental health and self-harm, you can also do the following (some I have repeated because of their importance):

1) Try not to panic or freak out as your teen is likely to pick up on your emotions and make the situation worse, as they may feel guilty for worrying you and shameful about their suicidal thoughts.

2) Get professional help from your GP and a counsellor or psychologist. It is paramount you find a therapist your teen connects with, or it is unlikely to help. If they are already engaged with a mental health professional, inform them of your concerns and consider increasing the sessions your teen has with them.

3) Encourage your teen to call the children's helpline if they need immediate support or someone to talk to between therapist appointments.

4) Be present and available for them to talk to whenever they need to. Make sure they know you will listen without judgement, and they can tell you anything.

5) Spend quality time with your teen and prioritise them. Meet them where they feel safe and comfortable; for example, go to their room.

6) Let them know you love them and how important they are to you.

7) Focus on the positives in your lives and do fun things together to help shift your teen's perspective and know there are things to live for.

8) Minimise conflict and negativity as much as possible within the household.

9) Know your teen's closest friends and their parents. Be in contact with them so you know what's going on for your teen, who their support network is, and if they have concerns for your teen.

10) Let the school know about your concerns and make a safety plan for school.

11) Get yourself support to process all the challenging thoughts, feelings, and situations that will arise.

12) Actively engage in your teen's therapy and healing process.

If you ever believe your teen is an immediate risk to themselves, you must call emergency services and keep them safe until they arrive.

Case Study: Sadie, 15 years.
(name changed for confidentiality)

The Struggle

Sadie lived with her parents and had an older brother. She was self-harming by cutting herself on the wrist and arm. She was also engaging in problematic risk-taking behaviour, drinking alcohol and smoking marijuana regularly. Sadie had low self-esteem and had experienced bullying in the past. She also attempted suicide by taking over-the-counter medication. She said she hid the extent of her mental health challenges and her self-harm from her parents for 2-3 years prior to them recently discovering what was going on for her. Sadie's parents struggled to support her and were scared for her safety. Sadie wouldn't talk to them about what was going on for her even after they found out. They attempted to send her to a psychologist, but she wouldn't engage.

The Transformation

Sadie was unable to explain or manage her feelings very well, which is why she self-harmed. She said it was her way of releasing the overwhelming emotions she had and helped ground her when she felt out of control. We worked on Sadie's emotional intelligence and used the emotions wheel so she could identify her feelings and learn to process them in healthy ways rather than cutting herself or using drugs and alcohol to self-medicate. I taught Sadie to incorporate exercises such as mindfulness, meditation, journaling, gratitude, grounding herself through the senses, and breathing to help her manage her emotions. I also worked on constructive communication so she could express her feelings and thoughts rather than keep them inside.

I helped Sadie find a psychologist she connected with and learnt to trust. It took a long while, but over time, Sadie began to heal, build her self-esteem and refrain from self-harming. She gradually stopped drinking and smoking and began treating herself with more respect. Sadie started to talk more to her parents about what was happening for her. Sadie made sure she continued to use the exercises I taught her and incorporated a self-care routine into her day.

Eating disorders.

Eating disorders are complex mental health and behavioural issues that affect a person's eating habits, their attitude towards food, and their self-perception about body image. These disorders can have severe implications for physical health and, in extreme cases, can be fatal. Although eating disorders are more common in females, the incidence among boys and men is rising more rapidly than in girls and women.

Adolescents are particularly vulnerable to eating disorders, with many of the beliefs and behaviours that lead to an individual developing an eating disorder in adulthood, first emerging during adolescence.

The DSM-5, the Diagnostic and Statistical Manual of Mental Disorders published by the American Psychiatric Association (APA), identifies three eating disorders that we commonly see in teens: anorexia nervosa, bulimia nervosa, and binge eating disorder. While orthorexia nervosa is not currently recognized by the DSM-5, it remains a concern for many mental health and eating disorder professionals, so I'm including it in this discussion.

Anorexia Nervosa

Teens with anorexia have an intense fear of gaining weight and a distorted view of their body. This means they believe they are fat even when they are extremely thin. A teen with anorexia will be very strict about their food intake and may fast or exercise excessively to lose weight quickly. They may use other methods to reduce their weight, such as taking laxatives or water pills or having an enema. It has the highest mortality rate of any mental health disorder.

How do you know if your teen is vulnerable to developing anorexia or if they already have it? Here are some signs:

1) They have a preoccupation with their body and weight.
2) They follow lots of pages and influencers on social media who are very thin and focus their content on their body and diet.
3) They look at Pro-ana (pro-anorexia) movement websites and forums, a subculture that encourages anorexia.
4) They count calories.

5) They skip meals.
6) They have considerably reduced their food intake.
7) They are obsessed with food content.
8) They have rules around food.
9) They don't want to eat around other people.
10) They have body dysmorphia, where they are extremely focussed on apparent flaws and defects in their body, which are usually unnoticeable to other people. They have persistent feelings of shame and anxiety about the perceived "flaw."
11) They have and/or are experiencing extreme weight loss.

Bulimia

Teens with bulimia will binge on food and feel an inability to stop eating. Then, they throw up, restrict their food intake, and/or use laxatives, diuretics, water pills, and excessive exercise to make up for it. They often hide their binge-purge cycles because of the shame around it, and their self-esteem is closely attached to their weight and appearance. Unlike teens with anorexia, those with bulimia may be of average weight or even overweight due to the amount of calories they consume during binges.

The following are signs your teen may have bulimia or is at risk of developing it:

1) They have a preoccupation with their body size, appearance, and weight.
2) They follow social media accounts that focus on exercise, diet, and appearance and who have the stereotypical ideal body shape.
3) They have body dysmorphia.
4) They hide food.
5) They eat secretively.
6) They overeat and ingest large quantities of food.

7) They eat quickly.

8) They have feelings of shame or guilt about food.

9) They have unconventional rules around food.

10) They go to the bathroom around or during meals.

11) They drink excessive amounts of water.

12) They take laxatives and/or diuretics.

13) They exercise compulsively and/or excessively.

14) They have marks on their fingers and knuckles from purging.

Binge Eating Disorder

Teens with binge eating disorder will overeat uncontrollably and consume large quantities of food even when they are full. They will often eat in secret, hiding their bingeing, and have feelings of guilt and shame about it. They often eat faster than normal and gain weight due to the high number of calories they consume. Teens who binge eat often have low self-esteem and show signs of depression. Teens with binge eating disorder will exhibit similar signs to those who have bulimia, however, they will not purge or use other methods to compensate for the binge.

Orthorexia Nervosa

Orthorexia is an obsession with healthy eating and results in a person cutting out entire food groups and only eating a narrow range of foods. They are fixated on the type and quality of food rather than the quantity. Teens with this eating disorder will often start by adopting healthy or clean eating practices, which progress into orthorexia as they get stricter rules around food, remove entire food groups such as gluten, dairy, processed foods, and animal products, and cut out foods with ingredients such as fat, sugar, and salt. Diet culture encourages clean eating, so it's easy for these distorted habits to develop and go unnoticed in teens with orthorexia.

Symptoms of orthorexia to look out for in your teen:

1) They have strong opinions about their food choices and are critical of other people's choices.
2) They have strict rules around food and are inflexible about them.
3) They follow people and pages on social media advocating for healthy eating, clean diets, and cutting out food groups.
4) They get anxious when they can't eat in alignment with their high standards.
5) They are constantly thinking about food and planning what they will eat, including before going to restaurants.
6) They pre-prepare meals.
7) They feel guilty when they don't eat within their strict guidelines.
8) They feel sick from "bad" foods.
9) They have high self-esteem when abiding by their healthy eating habits.
10) They experience mood swings and show signs of anxiety and/or depression.
11) They pull away from friends who don't align with their strict food requirements.
12) They avoid social situations in case they can't adhere to their rules around food.
13) They constantly research healthy foods.
14) They take supplements and vitamins.
15) They lose weight.
16) They are malnourished from cutting out entire food groups.

Eating disorders are a complex issue, and teens may develop one for many reasons:

1) Puberty brings on rapid physical changes that overwhelm them.
2) They feel out of control and use food to regain control or to cope with these feelings.

3) They have a negative body image due to the ideal physical representations they see in the media and messages they receive from society about how they should look.

4) They hear constant messages about dieting, food, exercise, and weight.

5) They feel pressure to fit in and belong to a peer group.

6) They use it to manage increasing levels of stress and pressure at school.

7) Adults in their lives role model negative body image and behaviours, and they internalise these messages.

8) They feel or are socially isolated.

9) They have low self-esteem and self-worth.

10) They have poor emotional regulation.

11) They have perfectionist tendencies.

12) Their parents have high expectations of them and standards for them.

13) Their parents criticise them.

14) They lack resilience.

15) They did not form a well-defined identity.

16) They have had or are currently experiencing big life challenges.

17) There is comorbidity with other mental health disorders.

18) They have experienced trauma, abuse, or neglect, including bullying..

19) They are an athlete, dancer, or gymnast at a high/competitive level.

20) They are a model or desire to be.

Due to their crucial developmental stage, teens need proper nutrition to function and grow. Therefore, eating disorders have serious health implications. Depending on the eating disorder, your teen may experience the following symptoms:

1) Malnutrition.

2) Bone and muscle loss.

3) Difficulty focusing.

4) Fatigue.

5) Insomnia.

6) Fainting.

7) Impaired cognitive functioning due to brain shrinkage.

8) Severe dehydration.

9) Dry skin and brittle hair.

10) Gum disease.

11) Tooth decay and tooth loss.

12) Permanent bone density loss.

13) Ulcers.

14) Amenorrhea (menstrual cycle stops) and possible infertility.

15) Low blood pressure.

16) Damaged vital organs such as the kidney and the heart.

17) Inflammation of and damage to the oesophageal sphincter and oesophagus.

18) Bowel issues.

19) Disruptions to day-to-day functioning.

20) Increased symptoms of other mental health disorders.

21) Sleep issues.

22) Fatty liver.

Eating disorders are extremely concerning. You must get professional help for your teen if you believe they have an eating disorder or are developing one. They will build a recovery plan to treat your teen's eating disorder and manage any concerning behaviours. Understand that recovery for your teen is a journey and doesn't happen overnight. Also, be prepared; they may need inpatient hospitalisation as part of their treatment.

But how else can you support your teen?

1) Take time to process what you have discovered or believe.

2) I know it's difficult, but don't blame yourself.

3) Get on the same page as your partner or their other parental figure on how to support your teen and address their eating disorder.

4) Speak to your teen about your concerns at an appropriate time. Explain why you think they have an eating disorder, but don't accuse or blame them as they may withdraw completely.

5) Ask them what they understand about eating disorders and their effects. They may not think anything is wrong or realise how detrimental it is to their body.

6) Be present with them. This may mean reducing your other commitments for a while.

7) Encourage them to develop more positive social media use.

8) Ask their permission to use a content monitoring app that will allow you to see any concerning activity with the understanding this is about their safety and not a violation of their privacy.

9) Suggest they journal their thoughts, feelings, and behaviours to "dump" and process them. It is also a good way of identifying any patterns, for example, triggers to a binge.

10) Help them increase their feelings literacy and emotional regulation so they can handle their emotions better and process them healthily (Chapter 6).

11) Work on constructive communication so they can communicate their feelings and needs clearly and assertively (Chapter 8).

12) Assist them in building their resiliency so they can manage life's challenges more effectively and bounce back from them faster (Chapter 7).

13) Help them improve their self-esteem and increase their self-worth.

14) Help your teen identify their values and see if an eating disorder aligns with these, for example, kindness and respect.

15) When appropriate, look at volunteering or doing another activity they can find purpose in.

16) Start a new hobby to take their focus off food and their weight. Make sure these activities aren't related to food, exercise, or their appearance, for example, learning a language or an instrument or starting art classes.

17) Let them know they are more than a body, that their body is the least interesting thing about them, and there are so many other wonderful aspects to who they are. Explore these other aspects of their personality and abilities with them.

18) Nominate a safe adult they can speak to if they don't want to tell you everything and who will keep their information private.

19) Consider talking confidentially to the school about your teen's eating disorder for both their safety and to help in their recovery. Discuss this with your teen.

20) Get support for yourself from either a professional or a trusted friend and focus on self-care.

21) Be open to engaging in family treatment, as research shows it is very successful in treating teens with eating disorders.

Struggles With Identity

Adolescence is a time for teens to explore themselves and form their identity. There can be huge psychological, emotional, and social consequences if they are "different" and don't feel a sense of belonging. Teens could feel out of place due to their gender identity, sexuality, race, or religion. They may be differently abled or neurodiverse, an introvert, or highly sensitive person. There are many reasons a teen may not fit in.

Feeling isolated and unsure about who they are can result in a teen developing addictions, eating disorders, and mental health illnesses. They are more likely to engage in problematic risk-taking behaviour and express suicidal ideation. When a teen doesn't feel like they belong, they can start to internalise this as being something wrong with them. It is really important they find their tribe and a place where they are accepted for who they are.

There are ways you can help your teen discover their identity, find a sense of belonging, and be proud of who they are:

1) Help them form a well-developed identity.
2) Build their resiliency so they have the strength to explore who they are and the ability to manage setbacks in this quest more effectively (Chapter 7).
3) Assist them in identifying their values so they can find friends and peers who align with them.
4) Encourage them to explore different hobbies, activities, and social groups to meet like-minded people.
5) Suggest they follow social media people and pages with different identities and beliefs. For example, if they question their sexuality, follow straight, lesbian, gay, bisexual, and queer influencers to see whose messaging and content align. There are also plenty of differently abled and neurodiverse social media profile pages.
6) Help them increase their self-worth so it is not attached to other people's opinions of them.
7) Send them the message that being different means they are unique, and it is to be celebrated.
8) Help them improve their emotional literacy, as they will have a lot of different and often confusing emotions come up while they are questioning who they are (Chapter 6).
9) Teach them to have strong boundaries and how to enforce them.
10) Help them with constructive communication so they're able to express their opinions, thoughts, feelings, and needs clearly (Chapter 8).
11) Check in with your teen regularly and be available for them to talk whenever they need in a safe and non-judgemental space.

12) Suggest they start a journal to help process any thoughts, feelings, and challenges around their identity. Make sure they include positive aspects of their identity and things they are grateful for.

13) Educate yourself and explore your teen's identity with them if they are open to this. For example, if your teen is adopted, learn more about their birth culture, find community groups, and visit their country or place of origin if possible.

14) It is a harsh reality, but your teen may be the target of discrimination, bullying, and verbal and physically aggressive acts just because they are different. It is important they learn how to protect and defend themselves safely. This could be having a personal alarm on them, learning about body language, taking self-defence classes, and understanding conflict resolution.

15) Role model being your authentic self for your teen so they know it is acceptable and empowering to be who they are (Chapter 9).

16) Make sure they know you love them for whoever they are.

17) Seek professional support for your teen if necessary. They must align with your teen's needs. For instance, find a counsellor from the LGBTIQA+ community if they are questioning their gender or sexual identity.

18) Understand that because your teen may be different from you or your expectations of them, it doesn't mean there is something wrong with them. For example, if your teen prefers to be alone and has one or two close friends, they may be an introvert or highly sensitive person, and you shouldn't force them to socialise or be concerned they don't have many friends. Talk to them about it.

19) Get support for yourself if you are struggling with your teen's identity and what it means for their future.

Case Study: Spencer, 14 years.
(name changed for confidentiality)

The Struggle

Spencer was the son of a single mum after his dad died two years prior to my meeting them. Spencer was questioning his sexuality and gender identity. He was wearing makeup and nail polish, of which his mum was supportive as she was happy for him to express himself in any way he wanted. However, Spencer was skipping school and causing a disruption in class when he was there. He wouldn't do his homework and was rebelling against the household rules. His mum was distressed and didn't know how to manage him.

The Transformation

I worked on constructive communication with Spencer and his mum to reduce conflict at home with the understanding something was going on with Spencer that he wasn't talking about, and his mum wasn't responding to his behaviour in the best way. Spencer admitted he was being bullied at school for wearing makeup and nail polish, which is why he was skipping school and being disruptive when he was there because he was defending himself against the bullies.

We worked on finding safe spaces where Spencer felt a sense of belonging, such as local LGBTIQA+ youth groups and online forums where he quickly formed new friendships with other kids in the community. His mom spoke to the school about the bullying, and they even looked at changing schools because Spencer wanted to go to school with his new friends. We worked on Spencer increasing his resilience as he is, unfortunately, likely to face more discrimination in the future. By increasing his resilience, Spencer will have a greater ability to manage challenging situations in ways that are not detrimental to his own well-being. Spencer was becoming happy with and confident in who he was and learning not to let other people's opinions undermine that. Spencer also decided he didn't want to constrain himself with labels, and his mum continued to be completely supportive.

Conclusion

Adolescence is a time when your teens' emotions can be intense, erratic, and tumultuous. They can be overwhelming, difficult to understand, and even harder to control. As your teen's brain lacks maturity, they are less able to use logic and reason when they face life's problems and respond more emotionally than an adult would. As such, these challenges can overpower them and result in your teen developing problems with their mental health as they find ways to mitigate their feelings and ease the tension within, such as controlling their food and weight, or self-harming.

Teens are already in a state of upheaval during adolescence as they are experiencing fundamental psychological, physiological, emotional, and social changes. They are discovering their identity and searching for their place in the world, so they often lack solid foundations. They can easily internalise their problems or perceived shortfalls and attach what's happening to them or around them to their identity, destroying their self-esteem.

However, there are also many protective factors and actions you can take as a parent to help your teen improve their mental health and progress successfully through adolescence. You can use any of the suggestions in this chapter that feel aligned with your teen and family to support them through an extremely difficult time. I won't pretend it will be easy because mental health is a complex issue and has many contributing factors, but it is absolutely possible for your teen to heal and thrive in life.

Furthermore, understanding mental health means you can help your teen address any addictive behaviours and other maladaptive practices at their root rather than tackle the symptoms, meaning they are less likely to relapse or replace one addiction with another. They can adopt healthy coping strategies that will serve them into adulthood and can move forward confidently, knowing they can face any challenges with strength and resolve.

SECTION 3

SECRET STRATEGIES FOR SUCCESS!

CHAPTER 6

We Are All Emotional Beings With Needs

"Emotions make the World go round."

Due to the developmental stage your teen is in, their brain isn't fully matured. As a result, they are more easily controlled and overwhelmed by their emotions. This inability to regulate their emotions effectively is a common factor in many of the problematic risk-taking behaviours teens engage in, such as drinking and drug use. It also contributes significantly to mental health illnesses, self-harm, and suicidal ideation. Therefore, it's fundamental for your teen's well-being to improve their emotional literacy and emotional regulation and to increase their emotional intelligence.

If your teen possesses emotional literacy, they will have the self-awareness to identify, name, and express their feelings in a healthy manner. Emotional regulation means they will be able to manage and respond to emotional experiences effectively, while emotional intelligence will equip them with the ability to manage their own emotions and to recognize and influence the emotions of others.

Emotional Literacy

Firstly, we need to know what feelings and emotions are. Although they are often used interchangeably and are connected, they are different phenomena.

Emotions (also referred to as primary emotions) are unconscious and arise as sensations in the body. They are the raw data and give a more accurate picture of an experience. It is important to understand that emotions are neither good nor bad and serve a purpose. How a person manages and processes their emotions can be healthy or unhealthy.

Feelings (also referred to as secondary and tertiary emotions) are conscious and occur in response to physical or emotional experiences. They are generated by thoughts and influenced by the stories we tell ourselves about a situation. Feelings are subjective and personal and can be changed. For example, your teen is being bullied. During an incident, the emotion would likely be fear because they are feeling threatened. But their feelings may be worthlessness, powerlessness, or self-hatred because they believe what the bully says is true.

The first step to improving their emotional literacy is for your teen to learn how to identify their emotions and feelings. However, this can be easier said than done, as the emotions they express may be concealing what they really feel. For example, your teen may appear angry because of their words, tone of voice, and body language, but in reality, they feel scared, embarrassed, or frustrated. However, it is unlikely they are self-aware enough to understand this is the case.

In this chapter, I will share Unique Parenting's Emotions Wheels. There are many emotion wheels available; however, through my work, I found most teens were overwhelmed by the sheer number of emotions and feelings displayed on a typical wheel. Therefore, I broke them down into separate wheels containing a single primary emotion and a maximum of 20 feelings. I also found many emotion wheels use colours that imply emotions and feelings are positive or negative, which can be detrimental to your teen's understanding of them.

For instance, anger is a healthy emotion as it can alert your teen to one of their boundaries being crossed, but it's how they process and display this anger that can be unhealthy. They may get verbally or physically aggressive versus confidently expressing their feelings to the person who crossed their boundary and assertively telling them not to do it again.

The Emotions Wheels

Dr. Paul Eckman is a psychologist who specialises in emotions and is the co-discoverer of micro expressions. He found there to be six basic emotions, which are anger, surprise, disgust, enjoyment, fear, and sadness. He later added contempt. I based Unique Parenting's emotions wheels on his six original primary emotions and built the wheels to include the secondary and tertiary emotions (feelings). Let's reiterate what emotions and feelings are in relation to the emotions wheels.

Primary emotions are the first and instinctive emotional response a person has to a particular internal or external stimuli, and you are born with them. They are usually less complex and provide information about the situation a person is in at the time. For example, your teen feels sad about arguing with their friend.

Secondary emotions (or feelings) are reactions to the primary emotions. For example, your teen may feel guilty because they did something to cause the argument. They can also be a method of self protection. Your teen may feel defensive because, deep down, they know the argument was their fault. Secondary emotions are learned.

Secondary emotions can be further broken down into tertiary emotions. In our example, if your teen is arguing with their friend, tertiary emotions can be remorse and shame for their actions. Furthermore, the six primary emotions can also be secondary responses. For instance, your teen feels lonely because they aren't seeing their friend due to their argument. Then, they feel sad, which is a primary emotion but a secondary response.

This may help explain why emotions are so complex and how increasing your and your teen's emotional literacy, emotional intelligence, and emotional regulation are fundamental to their well-being and success in life.

Figure 5.

Emotions Wheel

Using the Emotions Wheels

Unique Parenting has 12 Emotions Wheels, excluding the one displaying the primary emotions. These are:

Surprise Fear - 1
Anger -1 Fear - 2
Anger -2 Enjoyment - 1
Disgust Enjoyment - 2
Sadness - 1 Enjoyment - 3
Sadness - 2 Enjoyment - 4

Humans have a propensity towards focusing on negative thoughts, feelings, and events, a phenomena psychologists call the negativity bias. So, I think it is powerful to notice there are more joyful secondary and tertiary feelings than any of the other primary emotions.

Activity: This is an activity for you, your teen, and other family members to do.

It is very simple to use the emotions wheels. Find the emotion you think you feel on one of the wheels, then look at the other emotions and see if they align more with how you feel. Or do you have multiple feelings? For example, you think you feel surprised by something your teen tells you, but you actually feel shocked and confused. Your teen may think they are angry, but they are frustrated or actually overwhelmed (which is a feeling associated with a completely different primary emotion).

By making this practice a habit, you will both learn to become aware of your initial emotions and your subsequent feelings. Once you can identify and name your emotions and feelings, you can work on processing and communicating them. You will also be better at recognizing the emotions of others.

Also, try and tap into how the emotion feels in your body so you become aware of their somatic symptoms (bodily sensations). This will improve your ability to identify your emotions while you are experiencing them, which is an important step to managing them.

Activity: You and your teen choose some emotions from the emotions wheels and use them in a sentence during the day. For example, "I feel exasperated when I see litter all over the street when there are dustbins nearby." This helps expand the emotions and feelings you can name.

Figure 6.

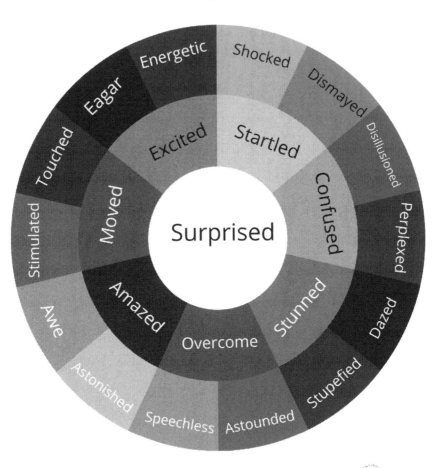

Figure 7.

Anger - 1

Figure 8.

Anger - 2

Figure 9.

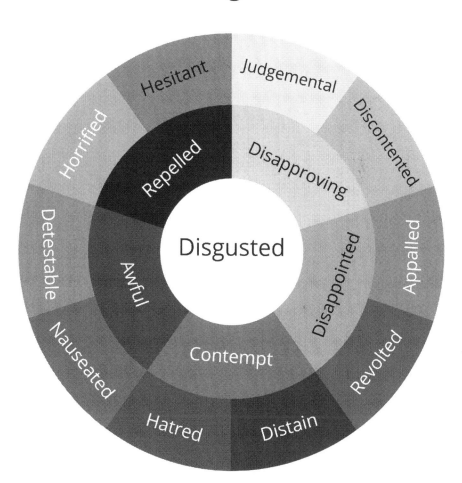

Disgust

Figure 10.

Sadness - 1

Figure 11.

Sadness - 2

Figure 12.

Fear - 1

Figure 13.

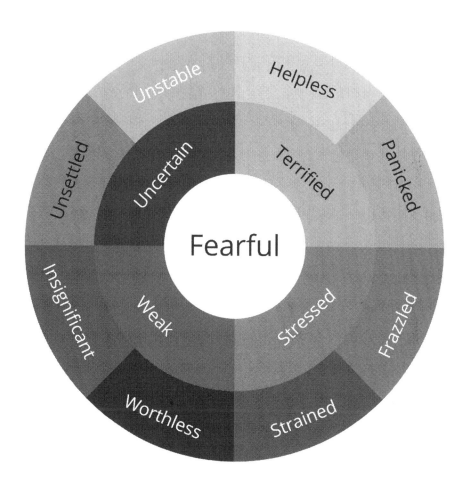

Figure 14.

Enjoyment - 1

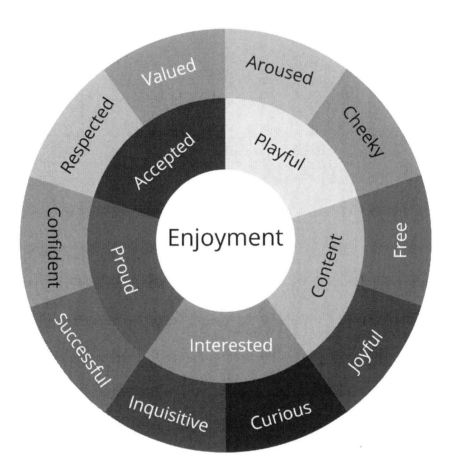

Figure 15.

Enjoyment - 2

Figure 16.

Figure 17.

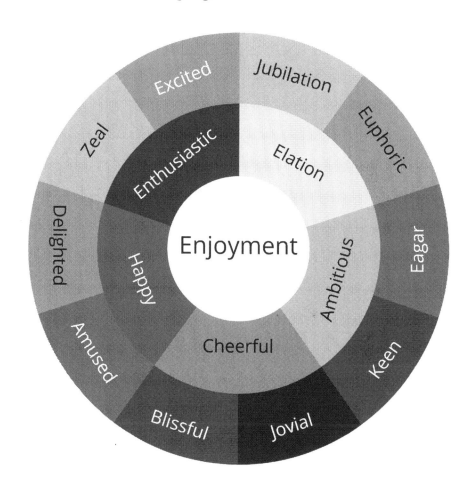

Emotional Regulation

It can be really difficult for teens to naturally regulate their emotions due to their brains being immature. The prefrontal cortex is, among other things, responsible for judgement and impulse control and is not yet fully connected in the adolescent brain. Because of this, teens must rely on their amygdala more than adults do, which is associated with emotions, impulse, aggression, and instinctive behaviour. This makes them both more emotional and less capable of managing them. To cope with their often overwhelming and confusing emotions, teens may turn to practices such as drinking, smoking, taking drugs, and self-harming.

They are also vulnerable to developing addictions and mental health illnesses. Therefore, teens must learn the skills to regulate their emotions in healthy ways. It will also benefit you and your relationship with your teen because you will be less triggered by their behaviour and more able to handle challenging situations effectively. The emotion wheels help you and your teen to identify and name your emotions, which then makes them easier to manage and process, which is where emotional regulation comes in.

Using the following practices, you and your teen will be able to manage emotional situations better and increase your capacity to experience a larger range of emotions:

1) Use breathing exercises such as diaphragmatic breathing and box breathing. In diaphragmatic breathing, you lie down and place one hand on your belly and one on your chest. Breathe deeply through your nose and into your belly so the hand on your stomach rises. Then, continue to breathe into your chest so your other hand rises. Slowly breathe out again and watch your hands descend. This type of breathing is shown to slow the heart rate and lower blood pressure. With practice, you can start to breathe this way during challenging

situations to calm yourself (obviously without lying down or needing your hands as guides). Box breathing is a practice used by the Navy Seals. You breathe in from the nose for four counts, hold the breath for four counts, breathe out from the mouth for four counts, and hold empty for four counts. This breathing can settle nerves and anxiety, decrease stress levels in the body, and calm the mind.

2) Put time between the trigger and your response. This could be focusing on a few deep breaths, counting to 10, or even walking away from the situation and re-engaging when you have calmed down (self-soothed). Make sure you tell the other person why you need space and don't just walk away, as this will likely escalate the situation.

3) Take the helicopter view. Imagine yourself pulling back and looking down on the situation as if you were in a helicopter. This removes you from the situation and distances you from your feelings, giving you a more impartial and clearer perspective.

4) You can use the five senses to ground yourself in the present moment. Name three to five things you can smell, hear, see, feel, and taste. Practise this technique during calmer moments so you can employ it when you are getting emotionally overwhelmed.

5) Use mindfulness. Mindfulness refers to staying in the present moment and having an awareness of your thoughts, feelings, your body, and the environment. It is done with an objective, non-judgemental, and self-compassionate lens. Being mindful makes you less likely to get caught up in thoughts about the past or future, which can lead to feelings such as anxiety and depression. It also enables you to stay calm during emotionally triggering situations.

6) Meditation is a mental exercise where you focus attention and awareness on one thing; it could be a thought, an object, or an activity. It induces feelings of relaxation and calms the mind. It helps reduce anxiety and stress and, with practice, enables you to remain centred during challenging times. Mindfulness is a form of meditation. Other

examples are movement meditation, visualisation, guided meditation, and sound meditation.

7) Get bored and sit with the uncomfortable feelings that arise. We all use distractions to avoid feelings, so getting familiar with them helps you learn to recognize and process them.

8) Shift your mindset around emotions. Emotions are "energy in motion." They are meant to be felt and released, not suppressed and locked inside the body, where they can fester and cause disease. It is often why people suddenly "explode" out of nowhere because they can no longer contain the build-up of unexpressed emotions and release them all at once.

It is important to honour all feelings, the comfortable and uncomfortable, the socially accepted and the less acceptable. We don't need to be happy all of the time. In fact, it's completely unrealistic and is known as "toxic positivity." Instead, let yourself and your teen feel the whole range of human emotions without judgement and release them.

Emotional Intelligence

Emotional intelligence (EQ) is having both the ability to recognize and manage your own emotions, having an awareness of other people's emotions, and the ability to influence them. EQ is a set of skills you and your teen can develop that will positively affect many aspects of your life.

1) *Mental health.*
   People with a high EQ typically have a more consistently positive mood, are able to recover from emotionally challenging situations more quickly, and bounce back from negative moods if they experience them. People with a low EQ have a higher risk of developing mental health disorders such as anxiety and depression. Increasing your teen's EQ will make them less likely to develop any of the mental health illnesses they are especially vulnerable to.

2) *Physical well-being.*

Stress can cause serious physical health issues, including digestive issues, weight gain, high blood pressure, sleep problems, and heart disease. A person with a high EQ has the ability to manage their emotions effectively, meaning they minimise their stress and the impact it has on their physical health. People with a high EQ also engage in better habits and don't rely on maladaptive coping strategies such as drinking and smoking to manage challenging emotions and situations. By your teen increasing their EQ, they will be less inclined to turn to risky behaviours as a way to cope with their emotions.

3) *Interpersonal relationships.*

Having a high EQ helps a person identify and manage both their own emotions and those of others. Your teen will be able to form healthy relationships and keep them. They will be less reactive and triggered by the actions and moods of others and have better control of their own when challenged in relationships.

4) *Social intelligence.*

Having a high EQ also assists in developing social intelligence, which is the ability to make sense of the people around them, know what motivates them, and informs them how to interact with others in social situations. In summary, it helps a person understand how to be part of a group. If your teen increases their EQ, they will be able to function better in social situations and know how to interact with different personality types in a range of settings.

5) *Academic achievement and work performance.*

A high EQ is positively correlated with a person's academic and work performance. They are more motivated and are better able to manage their emotions under stress. Improving your teen's EQ will assist them in managing their emotions under stressful situations, such as when they have heavy workloads, when assignments are due, and during exam periods. As such, their academic performance will be positively affected.

A number of traits common to a person with high EQ are:

1) *Emotional regulation.*
   They have the ability to recognize and manage their emotions.

2) *Self-awareness.*
   They're aware of and understand how their feelings, thoughts, and behaviours align with their internal compass and what makes them who they are.

3) *Self-confidence.*
   They have trust in their own judgement, skills, and abilities.

4) *Assertiveness.*
   They're able to communicate their point of view clearly and honestly in a direct manner and with respect for the other person.

5) *Social skills.*
   They can effectively recognize, manage, and influence the emotions of others.

6) *Empathy.*
   They're able to understand, identify with, and experience another person's emotions from their point of view as if they were their own.

7) *Adaptability.*
   They're flexible and embrace change.

8) *Prioritise progress over perfection.*
This enables them to be more productive and promotes learning as they go.

9) *Motivated.*
They are self-motivated and are driven by a personal desire for growth and achievement.

10) *Resilient.*
They're able to withstand, adapt to, and recover from difficult experiences and challenging life situations.

11) *Constantly learning and embracing feedback.*
They value growth and see feedback as a way to achieve this.

12) *Positive mindset and express gratitude.*
They have a more positive outlook overall and show appreciation.

13) *They live a balanced life and don't focus solely on one thing or another.*
They see the merit in and importance of all aspects of life, such as work, family, friendships, health, hobbies, and leisure time.

14) *They understand their needs versus wants.*
They can separate what is necessary from what is desirable and prioritise accordingly.

It is possible for your teen (and you) to increase your EQ by using the emotional literacy and emotional regulation exercises already discussed and by:

1) Noticing their self-talk and the stories they tell themselves about a situation. Is it true? This is a progressive step from the earlier exercise about identifying and naming their secondary and tertiary feelings that arise from their conscious beliefs.

2) Learning assertiveness skills and how to set healthy boundaries through constructive communication (Chapter 8).

3) Increasing resilience so they can handle stressful situations better and recover from setbacks faster (Chapter 7).

4) Improving self-awareness so they have an understanding of who they are, their emotions, and how they contribute to a situation (Chapter 9).

5) Focusing on self-care so they are less stressed and can manage challenges more effectively (Chapter 9).

Needs

Feelings are also a useful tool to identify if our needs are being met. The Cambridge Dictionary defines needs as "the things you must have for a satisfactory life." It is important for your teen to identify their needs, know how to meet them or ask someone else to meet them if they are unable. It is an extremely advantageous skill to develop during adolescence and carry into adulthood. Being able to communicate your needs effectively to others is also a core element of emotional intelligence.

Maslow's Hierarchy of Needs

A useful and well-known tool to help conceptualise what "needs" are, is Maslow's hierarchy of needs. Abraham Maslow was an American psychologist who proposed human motivation is driven by unsatisfied needs. Maslow started with the needs humans require to survive, such as food, water, and air. He then included other needs he identified as driving human motivation, such as health and well-being, connection, status, and purpose.

Maslow utilised a pyramid to show the progression from basic survival needs at the base to self-actualisation needs at the top, arguing a person struggling to survive will not be concerned with achieving self-actualisation. He proposed a person must mostly satisfy the needs of one level before progressing to and meeting the needs of the following levels. However, Maslow did acknowledge this process may not occur in a linear fashion due to the challenges and setbacks of life, meaning lower-level needs may need readdressing.

For example, if a person lost their job and subsequently their home, they would have to address the basic needs of shelter and employment, even though they had already met these needs previously. Such a loss is likely to also impact their feelings of self-worth and accomplishment, meaning they would have to work on fulfilling their esteem needs again in the future. It's worth noting that needs from different levels are often intertwined, and it's possible to address the needs of multiple stages concurrently.

Figure 18.

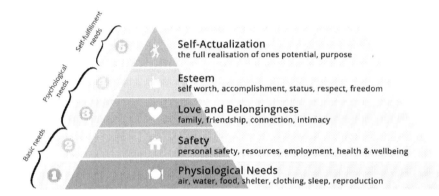

Maslow's Hierarchy of Needs Applied to Teens

Basic Needs

1) Physiological Needs: The most basic needs a teen has are biological needs such as air, clean water, nutritious food, a home, appropriate clothing, sleep hygiene, and good physical health. These needs must be satisfied if a teen is to meet their normal developmental physical milestones. Teens who are neglected often have these needs unmet.

2) Safety: It is important for teens to feel personal safety, have emotional well-being, a household with financial security, and a secure home environment. When teens feel unsafe, they are more likely to develop mental health illnesses and engage in addictive and problematic risk-taking behaviours.

Psychological Needs

3) Love and Belongingness: An important aspect of teen development is the need to develop interpersonal relationships and find a sense of belonging within social groups. A secure family unit is extremely important (in whatever form this takes) in providing a child's primary source of love and belonging. Then, during adolescence, teens prioritise the need to form strong friendship groups as part of discovering their identity. In later adolescence, they form intimate connections and explore couplehood. If a teen lacks a sense of belonging, they are more inclined towards problematic risk-taking behaviours and more vulnerable to mental health challenges and addiction.

4) Esteem: There are two categories

- Internally driven: It is an important and natural part of adolescence for teens to seek independence and engage in self-exploration. They need to find a sense of accomplishment within themselves and learn they are inherently worthy so their self-esteem remains healthy.

Internal esteem acts as a protective factor against many challenges teens face during adolescence.

- Externally driven: This refers to a teen's need for respect and recognition from others. This could include what their friends think about them, what their peers say to them, and the number of likes they get on social media. Although it is healthy to have a certain amount of externally driven esteem, teens who attach their self-worth to external forms of esteem have lower levels of self-esteem overall, an increased vulnerability to mental health illness, and are more likely to engage in problematic risk-taking and addictive behaviours. They are also more susceptible to peer pressure.

Self-fulfilment Needs

5) *Self-Actualization*: This can take a lifetime to achieve. For teens, it refers to setting and achieving goals, finding passion and purpose, identifying their values, discovering their skills, and seeking personal growth. Teens who are able to explore these have a stronger sense of self, well-developed identity, better mental and physical health, and are more resilient and successful.

Teens can use Maslow's hierarchy to help themselves identify their needs. They can start by using the needs he includes in his pyramid, then break them down further and expand on them. For example, one basic need is sleep hygiene. What do they need to get a good night's sleep? This may include a quiet and dark room, going to bed at the same time every night and waking at a similar time every morning, having no screen time an hour before bed, and not eating too late. All these are smaller needs necessary for them to meet the need for "good sleep hygiene."

Staying with this example, your teen can then delve deeper into what this need provides them and even discover their values. For instance, they need to sleep well so they have enough energy to train for and perform their best in their sporting game at the weekend. Here, they may have a need for physical health and community and discover values such as dedication, competition, and accomplishment.

Another example is your teen's need for belonging, under psychological needs on Maslow's hierarchy. What do they need to find a sense of belonging? This could include practical things like joining a youth group to meet people or having money to go to the cinema with their friends; learning social skills such as constructive communication so they know how to express themselves clearly within their friendships, and empathy to help connect with their friends at a deeper level and to maintain the bonds they form with them. By expanding on the needs for belonging, your teen may find they need respect and fun, and they have values around loyalty, honesty, and kindness.

Due to their developmental stage, teens require their parents or caregivers to meet their basic needs and assist them in meeting others. They also rely on community members to help them meet certain needs, such as teachers providing education. However, it is worth noting adults rely on others to help them meet many of their needs, too, because society is so interconnected. Adults are just more capable of meeting a larger number of their needs individually, specifically their basic needs.

Understanding Maslow's hierarchy of needs will also help you understand how to support your teen better. For example, if bullied, they will likely not prioritise school and their homework. This is because their basic need for safety is unmet, meaning they are unable to meet higher-level needs, such as esteem, under which academic success falls. So if your teen's academic performance falters, there may be an underlying issue, such as bullying, or they're struggling with their mental health and aren't just being defiant or lazy.

It is vitally important to help your teen find independence and learn the skills essential in adulthood for them to meet their needs, including the basic ones you are currently directly responsible for, such as providing food and a home, and indirectly, such as monitoring their physical and emotional well-being. Although you may think you are helping by doing everything for your teen, you are actually doing them a disservice because they will be unable to sufficiently meet their needs as an adult.

Furthermore, allowing your teen to struggle will help them to grow, just like diamonds are formed under pressure. But they need the right tools so as not to break. There is a sweet spot to work within as their parent, which is not always easy to find, but with resources such as this book and the techniques within it, you will have a greater capacity to do so.

Conclusion

Emotions are a complex and inescapable aspect of the human experience. Society values certain emotions, such as happiness, love, and courage, over others and teaches us to suppress those they deem as negative, such as anger, jealousy, and sadness. As a result, we often get overwhelmed by these "negative" feelings and manage them in unhealthy ways, particularly teens who don't have the same capacity to handle their emotions as adults do. Helping your teen increase their emotional intelligence will give them the ability to manage many aspects of life more effectively, preventing them from engaging in problematic risk-taking behaviours and developing mental health illnesses.

As feelings and needs are intrinsically linked, understanding their emotions will also help your teen understand their needs - they will feel good when their needs are being met and experience difficult and uncomfortable feelings when they aren't. Your teen can then fulfil these unmet needs themselves or ask someone else to meet them, something they will have the ability to do because of their emotional intelligence.

CHAPTER 7

The Building Blocks of Resilience

"Resilience is a superpower you can actually have."

As a parent, it's understandable you want to protect your children, but it's not always possible, especially as they grow older and become increasingly more independent. However, you can help them withstand difficulties, bounce back from challenges faster, and grow stronger as a result by helping them build resilience.

The American Psychological Association 2014 defines resilience as the process of adapting well in the face of adversity, trauma, tragedy, threats, or even significant sources of stress. Teens may experience a multitude of stresses and traumatic events during adolescence, such as the following:

1) Rapid physical, psychological, emotional, and social development.
2) Pressures from home life—chores, conflict, siblings.
3) Parental issues impacting them, for example, separation, divorce, redundancies, substance misuse, anger problems, and mental health.
4) Financial concerns—their own and/or their families.
5) Fear of letting loved ones down or not meeting expectations.
6) Grief and loss.
7) School life and academic pressures.

8) Partaking in and excelling at extracurricular activities.

9) Fitting in with peers and navigating friendships.

10) Forming and maintaining romantic relationships.

11) Sex, sexually transmitted infections, and teen pregnancy.

12) Identity formation.

13) Gender identity and sexuality.

14) Body image and self-esteem.

15) Social media.

16) Drugs and alcohol.

17) Gaming addiction.

18) Mental health, including anxiety, depression, eating disorders, self-harm, and suicidal ideation.

19) Sexual assault, physical assault.

20) Child protection concerns, neglect, abuse, poverty.

21) Bullying and cyberbullying.

This list may be confronting, and your teen will never experience them all, but I wanted to show you that teens are vulnerable to many life stressors you may be unaware of or minimise because they are "teens."

The Building Blocks of Resilience

The BBs of resilience is a framework by Unique Parenting used to understand the components of resilience and how you can help your teen build this valuable trait. The framework has seven components: autonomy, belonging, character, compassion, proficiency, purpose, and persistence. By developing these individual components, your teen will strengthen their resiliency and be more able to handle the challenges they face in healthy and effective ways.

1) *Autonomy.*

When your teen has the freedom and ability to make their own decisions, they build confidence in themselves and their competency in real-life situations. Taking responsibility and accountability for their decisions and actions is empowering. It means they have control over their lives and the way they respond to situations they encounter rather than passively accepting whatever happens. You can help your teen build autonomy by allowing them to make age and developmentally-appropriate decisions in their lives. Collaborate with them on guidelines that affect them, such as chores around the house, curfew, social media limits, and screen time.

2) *Belonging.*

A sense of belonging is fundamental to your teen's well-being and identity formation. When your teen belongs to various groups, they will feel secure and accepted, and with the support of those groups, they will have a greater capacity to manage challenging situations. They will also form a well-developed sense of self, have stronger values, and be less likely to engage in problematic risk-taking behaviours. You can help your teen find a sense of belonging by encouraging them to explore different relationships and friendships and by building a strong family unit where your teen feels safe and accepted for who they are.

3) *Character.*

Character refers to a person's values, morals, beliefs, and personality. Teens with good character have more self-confidence and higher levels of self-esteem. They have stronger values and morals, which they are more likely to adhere to and make better decisions on the whole. When they do make undesirable choices, they are more inclined to learn from them and not repeat them. You can help your teen build good character by encouraging them to seek a strong identity, thus forming a well-developed sense of self. You can role model what it means to have good character and foster these traits in your teen.

Figure 19.

The BB's of Resilience
(BUILDING BLOCKS)

4) *Compassion.*

Compassion is an emotion that arises when a person is sensitive to the pain of another and motivates them to help that person. Compassion can be felt in response to the emotional, physical, and psychological suffering of another and should also be felt for oneself. When your teen has compassion for others, it makes them more understanding of that person's situation and behaviours, and prevents them from taking their actions offensively. Also, by expressing compassion and helping those in need, your teen will feel good about themselves, which will increase their self-esteem. Furthermore, having self-compassion helps your teen maintain a more positive perspective during hard times and be more forgiving of themselves when they make mistakes. They will also have a greater sense of overall well-being. Your teen can build their compassion by increasing their emotional intelligence (Chapter 6), by adopting self-care habits, and by improving their self-awareness (Chapter 9).

5) *Proficiency.*

This refers to building the skills and competency to manage stressful and challenging situations. These skills include social skills and soft skills such as constructive communication, stress management, emotional literacy, emotional regulation, mindfulness, and self-awareness. Teens who have these skills are more able to handle stress, cope with the challenges of adolescence in healthy ways, and recover from setbacks faster. Your teen can build these skills by practising the methods discussed in this book, such as those around emotional literacy, emotional regulation, emotional intelligence (Chapter 6), constructive communication (Chapter 8), self-care, and self-awareness (Chapter 9).

6) *Purpose.*

Purpose is achieved through contributing to something greater than themselves. When teens make a difference in the world, it shows they matter. As a result, they will make more positive choices for themselves and others. They are less likely to develop mental health illnesses in response to difficult situations because they don't question their worth. Ensure your teen knows they have a purpose within the family unit and in the community. You can volunteer as a family or, if they can, volunteer for something alone. They could take on a social issue they feel passionate about and advocate for change. They could run for class president or another role at school. Or even help an elderly neighbour. No matter how small or large it is, having a purpose makes a huge difference to a teen's sense of self-worth.

7) *Persistence.*

Persistence is the ability to keep going in the face of challenges and continue trying when things get difficult in order to achieve a goal. Teens with persistence have the determination to strive for what they want despite adversity, meaning they are less likely to give up when they are faced with challenges or fall back on unhealthy strategies to cope with them. They would rather find solutions to problems and act even when it's difficult. Your teen can build their persistence by focusing on the process rather than the end goal and by reframing failure as learning. Keeping their values and "whys" in the forefront of their mind can also help them improve their persistence when things get tough.

Conclusion

It is extremely important for your teen to build resilience for a number of reasons. It will help them manage the challenges of adolescence more effectively, reducing the chances of overwhelm by helping them to maintain a more balanced life when under stress. It will assist your teen to overcome and recover from setbacks and hardships faster and more effectively. Resilience also works as a protective factor against developing mental health illnesses such as anxiety, depression, and eating disorders, engaging in risky behaviours, and falling back on maladaptive coping strategies such as alcohol and drugs.

CHAPTER 8

Conflict and Constructive Communication

"Conflict is communication done badly."

Communication often goes awry, but when it's done effectively, it can have phenomenal benefits in a multitude of ways. It can build relationships, strengthen existing connections, support growth, improve well-being, foster teamwork, increase academic and work performance, and more.

By understanding the reasons communication goes wrong and conflict arises, you can then communicate more consciously and considerably improve your interactions with your teen and, therefore, your relationship with them. Unique Parenting's "Complexity of Conflict" and "Constructive Communication" frameworks will both help you identify what's going wrong in your communication and remedy your approach so you and your teen can successfully navigate any challenging conversations with ease, walking away feeling heard, understood, and connected.

Although communication encompasses numerous mediums of exchanging, giving, or imparting information, here, I am referring to face-to-face communication.

The Complexity of Conflict

Conflict is when a serious argument or disagreement occurs over something meaningful to the parties involved and is often prolonged. Conflict can easily arise when two or more people communicate and prioritise their attachment to their needs and opinions rather than to seek understanding or find a resolution. Although conflict can be seen as healthy, I propose conflict isn't necessary because if communication is done well, people can have opposing needs and desires and convey them clearly and calmly while respectfully holding space for the other person.

I'm not saying arguments, disagreements, and debates aren't going to happen; they just needn't escalate into conflict. Conflict is a complex phenomenon and can occur seemingly out of nowhere. But with an understanding of how conflict arises, you can both reduce the likelihood of it occurring in the first place and prevent it from escalating if it does.

Unique Parenting's "Complexity of Conflict" framework was designed specifically to help parents and teens understand why conflict arises between them. It compiles factors into three categories: You, Your teen, and Environment. When you communicate with your teen, it isn't as simple as exchanging words. A huge range of factors influence a word's meaning and how it is processed by an individual versus that which the speaker intended. And, of course, the scenario gets a whole lot more complicated when multiple parties are involved.

Some factors contributing to miscommunication and conflict will be conscious, but a lot will be unconscious, as seen in Figure 20. In the Complexity of Conflict framework, the categories overlap and are intertwined, with factors associated with "You," "Your teen," and the "Environment" informing and influencing each other.

For example, you raised your teen and contributed to their beliefs. However, as they grow older, your teen will be influenced by other people, such as their friends and respected adults, and their beliefs will change and develop. You and your teen both live and function within an environment and, thus, are not isolated from its influences.

When you and your teen communicate, particularly about challenging topics, be aware of the factors below as they will impact the direction and level of success of your interaction:

1) Yours and your teen's vocabulary and understanding of it.
2) Your tone of voice and use of flexion. And those of your teens.
3) The body language you and your teen use.
4) Each other's understanding of what that body language means.
5) Your identity and theirs.
6) Both of your personalities.
7) Your beliefs and values. And those of your teen.
8) Both of your opinions.
9) Each other's desires.
10) Your past experiences and those of your teen.
11) Each of your understandings of the other's experiences.
12) Your triggers and theirs.
13) Any trauma each of you has experienced.
14) Your leadership role as a parent.
15) Your teen's role as your child.
16) Your expectations of your teen.
17) Their expectations of you.
18) How you and your teen feel emotionally—sad, stressed, angry, shameful.
19) Your ability and your teen's ability to regulate emotions.
20) Your emotional intelligence, and theirs.

21) How do each of you feel in your physical body? For example, are you tired or in pain?

22) Ego and identity are firmly attached to your opinions, beliefs, and desires. If you are wrong, it feels like a personal attack on your sense of self, and you become defensive, and conflict will likely arise. The same is true for your teen.

Figure 20.

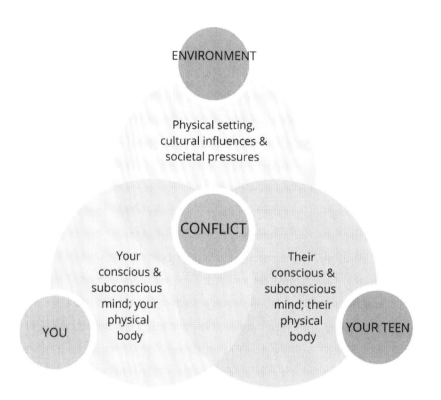

The Complexity of Conflict

ENVIRONMENT

Physical setting,
cultural influences &
societal pressures

CONFLICT

Your
conscious &
subconscious
mind; your
physical
body

Their
conscious &
subconscious
mind; their
physical
body

YOU

YOUR TEEN

Environmental factors also contribute to miscommunication and conflict. These can be grouped into three main categories:

1) *Physical setting.*

   This refers to where the conversation is physically occurring and the surrounding conditions. For example, in the car, their bedroom at home, in public. Is it noisy or quiet? Are there other people around, or is it just the two of you? Are you multitasking or completely focused on the conversation? As you can imagine, communicating in these contrasting situations will have different results.

2) *Cultural influences.*

   Culture is passed down between generations and includes the values, beliefs, behaviours, and traditions governing those who identify with that culture. These include examples such as a parent is always right, and they don't need to explain their decisions or that it is disrespectful for children to question their parents. Many cultures believe men and boys shouldn't show or express their emotions and women and girls should be placid and polite. All these impact the way a person communicates and what they talk about. There are certain things that aren't allowed to be discussed in particular cultures, and some behaviours and identities are unacceptable, therefore, remain hidden.

All these factors influence how a conversation unravels and will contribute to a person suppressing their thoughts, feelings, and opinions. This can lead to ill feelings such as resentment and result in conflict.

Reflect on your culture's attitudes and beliefs and how they may impact how you communicate with your teen—it needn't be negative!

3) *Society pressures.*

> Culture and society are different but intricately related. Society refers to a group of people living interdependently in a particular territory with common ways of living and, often, under shared political systems and laws. It includes the social structures and organisations of those in society. Although there is usually a dominant culture within a society, multiple cultures can coexist within it, making it culturally diverse.

There are numerous pressures on and expectations of you and your teen from society, which may impact your communication. You may not actually say what you want because it is not aligned with what society expects or dictates as a norm. This would include the opinions and expectations of other family members and friends. Furthermore, society often requires you to communicate in different ways in particular settings, depending on the person you are speaking with. For example, you wouldn't speak to your partner the same way you would to your employer.

It can be easy for your communication style to bleed into the wrong situation, such as speaking to your teen as you would your employees at work or the children you coach at swimming. Also, if you are raising your teen in a different society from where you grew up, there can be misalignment and confusion in your communication.

Finally, as you and your teen are from separate generations, you will also be experiencing society differently.

If you and your teen learn to use the Complexities of Conflict framework, you can apply it to any communication scenario by replacing "your teen" with any other person, for example, your partner, your colleague, your friend, or just "them." It would assist you both in having more effective and successful communication in other areas of your life. In Chapter 9, we will also look at how to limit the influence these factors have on your communication by finding your authentic self.

Constructive Communication: The Four Steps to Conflict-Free Communication

Now you are aware of why miscommunication and conflict arise so easily when you are having difficult conversations with your teen, you are better situated to implement Unique Parenting's "Constructive Communication" framework. The framework's guiding principles are based on communication as a whole, not specifically between you and your teen. The idea is to shift your perspective on communication overall, which will help you change your approach to communicating with your teen, which can be a naturally more charged experience.

The framework's guiding principles are:

1) *Communication begins in the mind and ends in the mind.*
   A conversation starts as thoughts in a person's mind before they become words. The speaker then expels words from their mouth in the form of sound, which enters the listener's ears to be processed in their mind. The cycle is repeated as the listener formulates their response. I know it seems obvious, but how often do you just focus on the words and not consider the conversation extends into thoughts? Most of the time, you are probably thinking rather than listening!

2) *Communication isn't about winning.*
   Conflict often arises because individuals are attached to their need to be right. When a person's identity is closely associated with their opinions and beliefs, they can feel attacked when someone has opposing ones. Their sense of self is threatened, so they need to "win" to solidify their identity.

3) *Communication is about understanding the other person better.*

By releasing the need to be right, communication is a phenomenal way to learn about another person and understand who they are. You can discover so much about a person by being curious, asking open-ended questions, and actively listening to what they say. Communicating with someone is also the only way you will truly understand their thoughts, feelings, and behaviours.

4) *Communication is about connection.*

When you understand a person better, you can connect with them on a deeper level and develop a greater sense of closeness. Honest and open communication will help you form and maintain relationships. Even if you have differences in opinions and beliefs, communication can be used to seek out connection instead of reinforcing separation.

5) *Communication is an opportunity to learn.*

If you enter a conversation with curiosity and openness, you can learn a lot about the world through other people. You can discover new facts and ways of thinking due to the other person's background, experiences, knowledge, and opinions. You will learn interesting and incredible things from engaging in conversation, particularly with strangers and people different from you.

6) *Communication is an opportunity for personal growth.*

Communication is a fantastic way to learn more about yourself and identify areas for growth. By receiving honest feedback from others, you can become aware of your strengths and weaknesses and choose to work on them. Additionally, you might discover new information and alternative perspectives that can broaden your understanding of a topic, possibly leading you to revise your beliefs and opinions.

Keep these guiding principles in mind when applying the Constructive Communication framework with your teen. As their parent, it's easy to forget many of these principles because you might feel you already know your teen so well. However, during adolescence, your child will undergo numerous changes in what they like and dislike, in their opinions, beliefs, and values, their friendship groups, and identity. Therefore, it's vital to view communication as an opportunity not only to understand them better but also for your own growth. It's an ideal way to connect with your teen as the individual they are becoming, not just the child you once knew.

The Constructive Communication framework comprises four main steps, each with its own four sub-steps. While it's especially beneficial for reducing conflict during challenging conversations, it can enhance the quality of any dialogue.

(refer to Figure 21.)

PLAN

- *Reflection*

   Reflect on the situation you wish to speak to your teen about. What are your thoughts and feelings about it? What are the facts, and why do you want to talk to them about it?

- *Preparation*

   Prepare what you are going to say to them, and start with the end in mind. What do you want to achieve by having the conversation? What outcome would you like? What information are you going to share with them?

- *Environment*

  Where is the best place to have the conversation? Where would you both be most comfortable, where there are no distractions? Does anyone else need to be present or should you be alone?

- *Timing*

  When is the best time to have the conversation? When you don't need to rush it or be interrupted, and when you both have the emotional capacity to manage it.

BE

- *Present*

  It is so important to be completely present during the conversation and truly listen to them instead of waiting to talk. This is where planning comes in because you won't be thinking about what to say, so you can focus on them.

- *Curious*

  Don't enter the conversation with preconceived ideas about the situation. Be genuinely curious about what they think and feel about it. Ask open-ended questions.

- *Authentic*

  Be genuine and true to yourself throughout the conversation. Keep aligned with your values, such as being a loving, supportive parent who wants the best for your teen.

- *Open*

  Be open to hearing what they say; you may not expect or like it. Your teen may also have a different view of the situation or side of the story to you.

SAY

- *"I" statements*

  Use "I" statements instead of "you" statements, which lay blame on your teen and will make them defensive, causing conflict. Reflect back on what you hear your teen say to make sure you have understood correctly, and ask questions to clarify if you are unsure. For example, "I hear you are feeling anger. Is that right?" rather than "you are angry." They might not be angry but frustrated, and assuming this can result in them getting defensive and/or withdrawing.

- *Feelings*

  Refer to how you feel about the situation and not accuse them of making you feel something. No one can make you feel anything; as such, they are yours to own and be responsible for. Name one or two feelings only. For example, "I feel disheartened when I see clothes all over your bedroom floor after I've asked you four times to tidy up."

- *Observations*

  Speak about the facts of what you saw or heard, and do not attach meaning to them. For example, "I saw you playing video games most of the day, and your room still has clothes all over the floor." Rather than accusing them of being lazy and selfish because they played their games all day and didn't tidy their room.

- *Requests*

Clearly ask for an action you want them to take and if they can do that for you. For example, "I would like you to put your clothes in the laundry basket when you are finished with them and tidy your room at the end of the day. Is this something you can do?"

DO

- *Negotiate*

If your teen says they cannot do what you ask, negotiate with them and ask what they are able to do. For example, they say they will tidy their room twice a week and would be more likely to put their clothes in the laundry if they had their own basket.

- *Win-win*

Collaborate with your teen to find a solution and get the best outcome for all where you are both satisfied and neither holds resentment.

- *Revisit*

Return to the conversation/topic to check how things are progressing and if you need to make any amendments to your prior agreement. For example, your teen agreed to tidy their room twice a week, but they are currently struggling with their school and extracurricular activities. Instead, while they are feeling pressure at school, they do it once a week and try to put things away as they use them.

- *Close*

Once you and your teen have discussed a certain topic and reached a resolution, "close" the matter. If necessary, you can gently remind them of the agreement, but treat it as a new engagement. This ensures you don't enter the conversation with a negative attitude and lingering unhealthy feelings, which would predispose you to conflict. For instance, instead of saying, "You promised me you would tidy your room, and you don't do it anymore…," start the process again from scratch. You can acknowledge your previous conversation and that the solution didn't work, renegotiate, and find a new solution.

Figure 21.

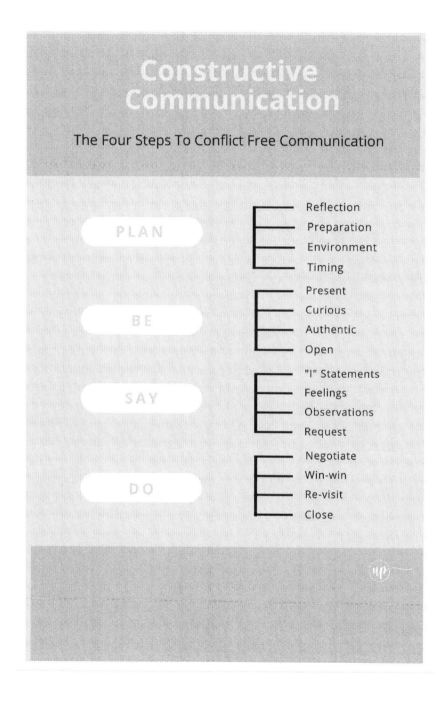

Conclusion

As we've discussed, communicating successfully with your teen is not as simple and straightforward as just speaking. There are a huge number of factors influencing the outcome of a conversation, which are exacerbated when it is challenging because one or both of you are likely to become offended and defensive. Furthermore, your teen is more emotional than you due to their brain development, and so will be more easily triggered. By being conscious of all the factors we have discussed and implementing the Constructive Communication Framework properly, you will notice a dramatic reduction in the frequency and intensity of the arguments between you and your teen, and your relationship will become stronger. Before you know it, using the framework will become second nature, and you will easily be able to apply it to any difficult conversation.

CHAPTER 9

The 3 Self's: Self-Care, Self-Awareness, and the Authentic Self

"Be healthily selfish!"

The Three Selves is a Unique Parenting framework designed around personal development. It has three stages: Self-care, Self-awareness, and the Authentic Self. The stages are interrelated and progressive, one helping inform the next. However, they are not necessarily linear, as life's challenges will knock you off balance and sway you between them. I'm going to show you how self-care is fundamental to your existence and is the first step to discovering who you are and unapologetically living in alignment with your true nature. By doing so, you will be a role model to your teen and give them permission to explore who they are. You will accept them unconditionally and empower them to unequivocally face the challenges of adolescence as their authentic self.

Self-Care

There's a lot of talk about self-care, and for good reason. It has positive impacts on pretty much every aspect of your life, including your sense of self, mental health, physical well-being, relationships, academic and work performance. I'm sure you will have heard the saying "fill your own cup" in reference to replenishing your own energy stores in order to give to others.

And the analogy of "putting your own mask on before helping others if the cabin pressure on a plane drops" which encourages you to prioritise your own needs. It's true, you'll most certainly be able to handle your teen's challenging behaviour more effectively if you are calm, collected, and full of energy.

First, let's look at stress and the impact prolonged stress can have on your well-being. Stress is a natural human response to perceived danger and triggers the body's sympathetic nervous system to prepare for fight-or-flight. It is a survival mechanism that evolved so humans (and other mammals) could react quickly to life-threatening situations and increase their chances of survival.

Two other stress responses have also been identified: freeze and fawn when fight-or-flight is not an option. "Freeze" mimics "play dead" in mammals and is when the body shuts down in the face of danger. In a person, it results in the inability to communicate, think or act. "Fawn" is employed as a last resort when someone will do anything to avoid danger or diffuse it, such as befriending their attacker. People who have experienced abuse often use this stress response.

Here, I will focus on the flight-or-fight responses.

The body has physiological and psychological responses to stress, preparing it to stay and fight or to flee the danger; some are noticeable, while others are hidden:

1) Hormones are suddenly released to activate the sympathetic nervous system.
2) These hormones stimulate the pituitary and adrenal glands to release hormones called catecholamines, which trigger the fight-or-flight response. These include cortisol, adrenaline, noradrenaline, and dopamine.
3) Your heart rate speeds up to increase blood flow to your muscles.

4) Your muscles tense in preparation for action, or they may shake and tremble.

5) Your hands will feel cold because blood is redirected to your major muscle groups to fight or flee.

6) Your palms will sweat, cooling the body to make it more effective.

7) Your breathing will get shallow and faster to draw in more oxygen for your muscles to use.

8) You may feel lightheaded or dizzy if you don't use the extra oxygen by fighting or fleeing.

9) You may feel the need to urinate as your bladder muscles relax.

10) Blood is diverted from the digestive system, so you may feel nauseous or have butterflies.

11) You will experience 'dry mouth' as another side effect of the digestive system shutting down.

12) Your vision will become more acute.

13) You will have racing thoughts and focus on the danger in order to make fast and life-saving decisions

The issue with this life-saving response to danger is that in modern-day society, we perceive threats everywhere, and our fight-or-flight response is constantly being activated by physical and psychological situations. There are obvious, massive life events that cause chronic stress, such as losing a job, chronic illness, death of a loved one, and other traumatic events. However, our interpersonal relationships, household obligations, school and work pressures, and financial problems all cause stress in numerous ways. We fear being judged and of failure, of not doing enough and frantically trying to "have it all."

Even stepping outside of our comfort zone can trigger our fight-or-flight response, and as a parent, you take on all the added stress of your teen and the real or perceived dangers they face. Now you are aware of them and can spot the signs, note how often you are experiencing stress. I bet it is more than you thought.

As our bodies are only designed to stay in fight-or-flight for short periods of time after the danger has passed, chronic stress can have serious detrimental effects on our mental, emotional, and physical well-being, including:

1) Irritability and mood swings.
2) Feelings of overwhelm.
3) Depressive symptoms.
4) Anxiety.
5) A pessimistic outlook.
6) Issues with anger and aggressive outbursts.
7) Feelings of restlessness.
8) Lack of motivation.
9) Lack of concentration and inability to focus.
10) Changes to appetite—overeating or undereating.
11) Increased drug and alcohol use.
12) Reduced physical activity.
13) Becoming socially withdrawn.
14) Increase in nervous habits.
15) Impacts judgement.
16) Headaches and migraines.
17) Chest pain.
18) Increased risk of stroke and heart attacks.
19) High blood pressure.
20) Heartburn.
21) Fatigue and listlessness.
22) Tension and/or pain in the muscles.
23) Sleep disturbances and insomnia.
24) Stomach and gastrointestinal issues.
25) Compromised immune system.

26) Increases risk of type 2 diabetes.

27) Erectile dysfunction and impotence.

28) Loss of libido.

29) Fertility issues.

30) Irregular or missed periods.

31) Increases prenatal health risk to both mother and baby.

I'm sure you now realise the importance of addressing and managing your stress. This is where self-care comes into play. Self-care engages the parasympathetic nervous system, which calms the body after a stress response. It reduces the number of situations you perceive as threatening, helps you handle stressful situations more effectively, decreases the intensity and duration of your stress responses, and mitigates the effects of stress.

Moreover, when you aren't constantly in fight-or-flight mode, you'll be more inclined to see the positive aspects of life, be able to focus on personal growth, and address any issues with your teen. I won't delve deeply into which specific self-care habits you should adopt, as what works for one person might not work for another; what nourishes and rejuvenates you will likely differ from what nourishes and rejuvenates me. However, I will help you reframe your understanding of self-care and emphasise its nature as non-negotiable.

There is a wider understanding of self-care beyond the massages, bubble baths, cups of tea, and walks in the park that need to be embraced. Self-care involves engaging in any activity that improves your quality of life and well-being and enables you to grow as a person.

There are eight dimensions of self-care and wellness commonly referred to by professionals in the well-being sphere. These are emotional, physical, spiritual, psychological/intellectual, social, financial, environmental and occupational.

Here are some examples of each dimension.

1) *Emotional.*

Developing and maintaining healthy emotional responses to life. Start a gratitude Journal, use positive affirmations, pet a dog, watch a funny film.

2) *Physical.*

The importance of physical activity, nutrition, and good sleep. Exercise, cook a nutritious meal, take a nap, have a bubble bath.

3) *Spiritual.*

Finding a sense of purpose and belief in something more. Meditate, practice mindfulness, go to yoga, pray, do a random act of kindness.

4) *Psychological/intellectual.*

This is about expanding your knowledge and understanding and learning new skills. Read a book, learn a language, play an instrument, journal, go to therapy.

5) *Social.*

Recognizing the importance of having a sense of belonging and building strong social networks. Offer to help a family member, go out with a friend, have a walk with a neighbour.

6) *Financial.*

Developing healthy spending habits and financial literacy. Save for something you really want, track your spending in an app, address mindset blocks around making more money.

7) *Environmental.*

Living and occupying spaces that stimulate and nourish you. Get some plants for your home, clear out your cupboards, hang some art.

8) *Occupational.*

> Finding enjoyment, satisfaction, and purpose in your work. Take time out for lunch, don't make work calls after hours, ask colleagues for assistance when you need it.

Figure 22.

Activity: You and your teen identify self-care habits for each of these areas. Then, pick two or three self-care practices to incorporate into your life (don't attempt them all at once) and maintain them for a month or so until they become habitual. Then, introduce another two or three. Not all practices need to be conducted daily, weekly, or long-term. For instance, a Financial Self-Care Act might involve a short course on financial literacy over 12 weeks. Once completed, it's accomplished. It's also worth noting that while some self-care habits will remain consistent, many will evolve as we grow and change. Thus, it's crucial to regularly reflect on the efficacy and relevance of your habits.

One challenge with self-care is that it often gets sidelined precisely when it's needed most. When burdened by time constraints, stress, distractions, or significant life events, self-care gets forgotten. However, those are the times you should prioritise it the most. The solution? Recognize that self-care is non-negotiable and embed it into your daily routine until it becomes habitual.

Self-care is a necessity, not a luxury. Without it, functioning optimally in daily life becomes challenging. Schedule it like you would an important meeting or a medical appointment. Shift your perspective on self-care: see it not as an occasional treat but as an essential part of maintaining well-being.

It's important to remember that self-care isn't about perfection. It's about consistently taking actions that enhance your overall well-being and enjoyment of life. It emphasises mindfulness. So, yes, savour that glass of wine. Fully immerse yourself in the sensory experience. That's self-care, as opposed to resorting to alcohol as a coping mechanism.

If you find yourself neglecting self-care practices, question what's hindering you. What obstacles are you facing? Is it a lack of time? Reflect honestly on this. Consider the hours you spend on Netflix or your phone. If other people seem to be the barrier, involve them in your well-being routines. If a particular activity doesn't appeal to you or you find yourself procrastinating, replace it with something you genuinely enjoy, and you're more likely to do it. Self-care should enhance your well-being, not induce stress.

When grappling with challenges related to your teen's behaviour, start by asking, "What can I do for myself?" Determine what's necessary to rejuvenate yourself so that you're better equipped to support your teen. You can't be of help if you're exhausted, stressed, or spread too thin. By focusing on self-care, you also set a positive example for your teen during this pivotal and challenging developmental phase. Introducing them to self-care early on helps protect against potential mental health issues, addictive behaviours, and problematic risk-taking behaviour. By emphasising the importance of self-care during their formative years, they're more likely to internalise these habits and carry them into adulthood.

Self-Awareness

Another thing self-care will do is teach you what you want and need. Also, to instil good self-care practices takes self-awareness. So, the more you discover about what nourishes you, the more you understand who you are and why.

There are two types of self-awareness. Internal self-awareness is the discovery of your values and beliefs and the process of becoming conscious of your thoughts, feelings, and behaviours, and how they align with your internal compass. External self-awareness is having an understanding of how other people perceive you.

Self-awareness is a continuous, lifelong practice that can be uncomfortable and challenging. However, it comes with huge benefits because self-aware people:

1) Have better mental health.
2) Have better physical health.
3) Are more flexible and adaptive.
4) Are more objective about themselves.
5) Understand and accept their limitations.
6) Are able to evaluate their behaviours against their values and align them.
7) Are able to regulate their emotions.
8) Have higher emotional intelligence.
9) Have higher levels of social intelligence.
10) Are more resilient.
11) Are better decision makers.
12) Have higher self-esteem and self-confidence.
13) Have better leadership skills.
14) Have stronger interpersonal relationships.
15) Have a better overall perspective.
16) Are more self-motivated.
17) Have more self-control.
18) Are more intuitive.
19) Are better communicators.
20) Are more empathic.
21) Are more creative and innovative.
22) Are more aligned with their skills and passions.
23) Are more successful.
24) Are more likely to act in socially acceptable ways.
25) Have deeper spiritual connections.
26) Are more focused on personal growth.

So, how can you and your teen increase your self-awareness besides engaging in the self-care practices we have discussed?

1) Refer back to feelings literacy exercises to help you bring awareness to your emotions (Chapter 6).

2) Journal your thoughts, feelings, and experiences to uncover any patterns.

3) Be conscious of your body language and posture and how it makes you feel. Do you feel more confident when you are slouching and "small" or standing tall with your shoulders back and taking up space? Do you feel happier when you have your head down, gaze low, and are marching through the street, or when your head is held high with a smile on your face, your steps slow and methodical?

4) Identify your values and why they are important to you. Then, measure your thoughts and actions against them and start to align them.

5) If you do something that doesn't align with your values, reflect on why.

6) Practice mindfulness, as this brings you into the present moment. Focus your awareness on the five senses—what can you see, hear, smell, touch, and taste?

7) Meditate and be curious about what arises for you—your thoughts, feelings, and bodily sensations. Observe them without judgement, then release them.

8) Ask for feedback and honest opinions about different aspects of your life from trusted people. This will help you understand yourself from other people's perspectives.

9) Be alone and date yourself. Learn about yourself.

10) Get bored and witness all the uncomfortable feelings that come up.

11) Make it a practice to reflect on things that go wrong and how you might do them differently next time.

12) Identify what your areas of strength and weaknesses are. You don't need to improve them if you don't want to, but be aware of them and acknowledge them. Accept you aren't great at everything because no one is.

13) Learn a new skill and experience a beginner's mindset, as this is something we rarely do as adults.

14) Do things out of your comfort zone and see how you respond.

15) Identify what challenges you about other people and see if you have any of these traits yourself.

16) See a therapist and talk. You'll be amazed at what you discover.

It needs to be said that self-awareness can have its disadvantages, though. It can make a person self-conscious and care too much about what other people think of them. It can lead to overthinking and overanalyzing. Some people even develop an inflated sense of importance. However, the final self in the framework can help prevent these disadvantages from becoming an issue.

The Authentic Self

The authentic self may sound esoteric and something only the spiritual and hippies talk about. But it is the doorway to achieving the life you truly desire. When you are your authentic self, you accept all of who you are without any guilt or shame. Your authentic self is who you are at your core, the person beyond the roles and labels you have adopted or society has imposed on you.

Activity: Take some time to reflect on these questions:

- How often do you hide behind masks, fearful the world would judge the real you? Think of some occasions you played a role instead of being your true self. Why did you feel you had to hide the real you?
- How many times do you act according to others' expectations of you rather than do or say what you really want? Explore some reasons why.
- How many people know the real you? Who are they, and why do you feel comfortable sharing your true self with them?
- Who can you share your quirkiest, darkest, most insecure parts with without fear? Why them?

Don't be concerned if you can't think of anyone for the last two questions; many people I have asked can't. This is a reflection of society, not on you. But it shows why finding your authentic self and living in alignment with it is so important.

So, what are the signs and consequences of living out of alignment with your authentic self?

1. You seek external validation.
2. You rely heavily on other people's advice and guidance.
3. You are constrained by fear of other people's opinions.
4. You engage in risky or addictive behaviours.
5. You constantly put others' needs before your own.
6. You burn out because you show up for others even when you don't have the energy to do so.
7. You are a very different person, depending on the situation.

8. You have unfulfilling or toxic relationships with partners who aren't right for you.
9. You have low self-esteem and self-confidence.
10. You are lonely, even when you are surrounded by others.
11. You are consistently stressed.
12. You have anxiety in case you do or say the wrong thing.
13. You have feelings of depression from living out of alignment with your values.
14. You get sick a lot.
15. You are in a job you don't like.
16. You procrastinate a lot and struggle to make decisions.
17. You feel resentful and taken for granted.
18. You have body image issues.
19. You have largely extrinsic values.
20. You don't know what you like or what your opinions, values, and needs are.
21. You find it difficult to communicate your opinions, needs, and desires.
22. You have "shallow" or surface-level friendships and relationships.
23. You are judgemental or critical of others.
24. You take criticism and judgement from others personally.
25. You suppress your dreams.
26. You believe others are responsible for your emotions and behaviour.
27. You think other people need to change.
28. You are different when you are alone to when you are in company.

It's extremely brave to be your authentic self and risk being judged or rejected by others. You will feel exposed and vulnerable, and it will likely trigger anxiety as you step outside your comfort zone, away from the familiarity of pleasing others. As you shift and strengthen your boundaries, you will likely lose friendships and have pushback from loved ones. But the payoff is incredible if you sit with and pass through the uncomfortable:

1. You won't engage in risky behaviour or addictive practices.
2. You will be very self-aware without being self-conscious.
3. You will have fewer friends but with deeper connections.
4. You will prioritise your own well-being.
5. You will know what your opinions, feelings, needs and desires are.
6. You will clearly communicate your opinions, feelings, needs and desires.
7. You will be more accepting of others.
8. You will have better mental health.
9. You will have better physical health.
10. You will have more energy.
11. You will have genuine romantic relationships with more intimacy.
12. You take accountability for your own thoughts, feelings, and behaviours.
13. You will know you are not responsible for anyone else's thoughts, feelings, and behaviours.
14. You will consistently be the same person.
15. You will know your values.
16. You will have more intrinsic values.
17. You will act in alignment with your values.
18. You will consider your own needs as well as the needs of others.
19. You will be self-confident.
20. You will have a positive body image and self-image.
21. You will rely more on internal validation.
22. You will find more fulfilment in your current work or seek more fulfilling work.
23. You will be more motivated.
24. You will have a sense of peace.
25. Your inner and outer selves will align.
26. You will be constantly growing and learning.

If this sounds great, here are some ways to become aligned with and live as your authentic self.

1) *Explore your values.*

You need to know your values to live in alignment with them. They will be your north star (an extensive values List is included in the Free Resources Bundle).

2) *Discover your needs (Chapter 6).*

What do you need to live a fulfilled life? Not want. These will likely be associated with your values.

3) *Do a life audit.*

Honestly, reflect on aspects of your day-to-day life and whether they add to your well-being or detract from it. Include areas such as sleep, nutrition, exercise, stress levels, self-care, and family and work responsibilities. Do they reflect the actions of the person you want to be? (a Life Audit is included in the Free Resources Bundle.)

4) *Journal.*

In a journal, you can be totally honest without fear of judgement. Note your thoughts, feelings, behaviours and unpack them. Are they aligned with your values? When do you feel most like yourself? Which people, places, and activities make you feel the happiest and most satisfied? Which do the opposite? If you haven't acted in alignment with your values, why? What purpose did it serve you?

5) *Act with integrity.*

Act in public as you would in private when no one is watching.

6) *Increase your emotional intelligence (Chapter 6).*

You will become more aware of your emotions and be able to express them. Your emotions are also great signposts to whether you are living in alignment. Are you feeling stressed, depressed, resentful, or angry rather than joyous, carefree, excited or enthusiastic? Alignment with your authentic self feels great!

7) *Improve your resiliency (Chapter 7).*

This enables you to stay strong in your authenticity when you are questioned and challenged by others or feel it is easier to just go with the majority instead of remaining in alignment with your values, desires, and opinions.

8) *Work on your constructive communication (Chapter 8).*

This will enable you to speak your truth honestly, confidently, and assertively. You will be able to ask for your needs to be met and make requests of others. You will be able to express your boundaries and say "no" without an explanation or feelings of guilt.

9) *Focus on self-care (chapter 9).*

Self-care will help you discover your needs and how to meet them. It will teach you to nurture yourself and prioritise your well-being. It will help prevent you from regularly sacrificing your own needs for those of others.

10) *Increase self-awareness (chapter 9)*

Self-awareness is a prerequisite to finding your authentic self. You need to discover who you are before you can live in alignment with it.

11) *Find your tribe.*

Form friendships and relationships with people you have a genuine, deeper connection with based on your core values and who you are/want to be. They will provide a safe space for you to be vulnerable and thus encourage you to live in alignment with your authentic self. These relationships will feed, nourish, and support you when things get challenging.

Becoming your authentic self is an ongoing process, and it doesn't happen overnight. However, the journey brings self-discovery, the challenges lead to growth, and exploring options offers satisfaction. With every step, you will learn: what you desire and what you don't, what aligns with your essence and what doesn't, and who you truly are versus who you show the world.

Becoming your authentic self will make you a better parent and role model for your teen. You'll demonstrate the value of having a well-defined sense of self. You'll teach them the significance of being the protagonist in their own life story rather than a supporting character. You'll empower them to be true to themselves and to love that genuine self without reservation. As you wholly accept yourself, you'll also embrace your teen for who they truly are, not merely as a reflection of your expectations.

It is invaluable to gift your teen the understanding of authenticity at this stage in their life. It's more accessible now, in their youthful years, characterised by risk-taking, thrill-seeking, and innate curiosity, and during their quest for autonomy and belonging. It's decidedly less daunting now than it will be later when they might be cloaked under layers of societal roles, labels, and externally imposed expectations. This understanding will fortify them against life's challenges and guide them along a path resonating with their core values and purpose. Consequently, they'll achieve greater success, form and sustain healthy relationships, and enjoy heightened levels of well-being. Their journey through adolescence and into adulthood will be one of joy, fulfilment, and adventure.

Figure 23.

The ③ Self's

Self-Care

Self-care is a non-negotiable & must be prioritised.
It is fundamental for a persons well-being & life satisfaction.
It encompasses much more than the narrow definition commonly used.
Through self-care you will learn more about yourself, your desires & whats important to you.

Self-Awareness

Self-awareness is knowing who you are & why. It is an understanding of your thoughts, emotions, behaviours, values & beliefs.
Being self-aware transforms the way you show up in the world for yourself & others.
Self-awareness is a continuous and life-long process.

Authentic Self

Your authentic self is who you are at your core.
You completely accept all aspects of yourself - the good, the bad the ugly - without shame.
You have the courage & confidence to show up as your true self, not as others want or expect you to.
Your inner & outer world align.

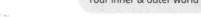

CHAPTER 10

The Power of Perspective.

*"It is far simpler and more effective to change your
thoughts than seek to change their behaviour"*

It can be really difficult when your teen constantly challenges you by the way they speak to you or behave. It is a natural part of adolescence to question authority, push boundaries, and seek independence, so the more you tell your teen to do something, the less likely they are to do it. And I'm sorry to say, you can't "make" them do anything. You can threaten them and punish them, but there are greater chances your teen will rebel, deceive you, and pull further away. So what's the answer? Change the way you think.

In 1985, Rosenthal and Bubbad said, "When we expect certain behaviours of others, we are likely to act in ways that make the expected behaviour more likely to occur." The work of Rosenthal and Jacobson in 1968 showed teachers' expectations influence student performance. The students who teachers expected to excel academically did, and those they deemed less capable achieved lower grades. Rosenthal and Jacobson described the psychological phenomena as the Pygmalion effect.

Another phenomenon, the self-fulfilling prophecy, agrees. When a person has expectations of someone else, it can lead to that other person behaving in ways that confirm their expectation. The self-fulfilling prophecy can either be "other imposed," like the Pygmalion effect, or "self-imposed."

Let me give you an example of self-imposed. You may have been told you were naughty growing up. You got told this enough that you started to see yourself as naughty and gradually adopted it as part of your identity. You did the "naughty things," such as playing up in class and bullying your younger sibling, confirming other people's view that you are naughty.

These psychological phenomena may help explain your teen's current behaviour. What expectations do you have of your teen? Do you see them as productive, intelligent, funny, and kind, or as lazy, stupid, argumentative, and moody? It also helps explain why someone else may have a completely different experience of your teen than you do; they have contradicting expectations of them. Your perception has a real-life impact on their behaviour and what you believe materialises in the world. You see what you look for. So if you change your perception of your teen, you change your lived experience, and you influence their behaviour. You really can improve your teen's behaviour by thinking differently.

Also, by seeing your teen differently, they will start to see themselves differently. They will incorporate your positive view of them into their identity, helping improve their self-esteem, self-confidence, and self-belief. And, as they align their identity with your more positive perspective of them, they will be less likely to engage in risky and addictive behaviours as they don't associate such actions with who they are.

As Figure 24 shows, you don't need to change your perspective overnight, which would likely be impossible. Instead, make minute shifts in your perception. These will accumulate over time, leading to radical changes in their behaviour.

Figure 24.

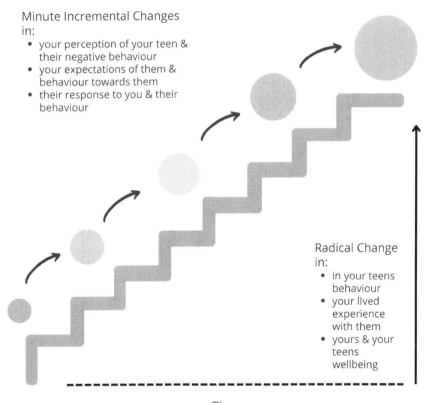

How a Small Change in Your Perception Leads
To Radical Change in Your Teens Behaviour

Minute Incremental Changes in:
- your perception of your teen & their negative behaviour
- your expectations of them & behaviour towards them
- their response to you & their behaviour

Radical Change in:
- in your teens behaviour
- your lived experience with them
- yours & your teens wellbeing

Time

Here's an example of how this works using Unique Parenting's MINDSET acronym to remember the process.

M = mindful.

You need to be present so you don't fall naturally into your old patterns of thinking. I wouldn't recommend trying this when you are tired, stressed, busy, or distracted because you likely won't get the outcome you desire.

I = Identify.

N = negative behaviour in your teen.

Think of a behaviour your teen exhibits that you find challenging. Say they're constantly questioning you and won't do as they're told. You get frustrated with them, your tone changes and your body language becomes standoffish toward them to prevent yourself from escalating (this is often subconscious). Your teen picks up on your energy and is less likely to do as you ask.

D = deciding on taking a new perspective.

Make a conscious decision to change your perspective about your teen's behaviour. It won't necessarily be easy, particularly if it's been an issue for a while.

S = see positivity in their behaviour.

Reframe their behaviour. What could the positive be in their behaviour? For example, questioning everything is often a sign of intelligence. And how might these traits be useful to them in their life now or in the future? How could they channel it for growth? For example, could they join the debate team or volunteer for the school newspaper to feed their curiosity?

E = expect something different.

You don't need to consciously act on this or even rationalise it. If your teen questions you when you ask them to do something, just say to yourself, "It's because they're intelligent." This small shift in your perception will influence your behaviour, impacting the subtle cues you give off through your body language, tone of voice, and energy. Your teen will pick up on this and respond ever so slightly to the change in you with their behaviour, to which you will shift your perception again and think more favourably of your teen. Your actions towards them change to align with your new perspective of them, and in turn, the behaviour changes for the better. The cycle repeats.

T = time.

Give it time. The process will be a gradual one, a dance between you and your teen. This may happen tens or hundreds of times. Minute shifts in perception and behaviour, and expectations and actions until your teen isn't the frustrating, defiant kid you once saw them as.

Activity: Write down all the big and little things you admire and love about your teen. Include aspects of their personality, such as their kindness and sense of humour. Consider their mannerisms and gestures, like the way they talk with their hands. Reflect on the behaviours you admire in them, for instance, how they play with their younger sibling. Think about their values, such as honesty and generosity. Recall their efforts, such as participating in a sponsored run, and their achievements—being a school prefect or winning a maths award. Remember their skills and talents, like art and dancing. Write down anything that comes to mind, and let it flow naturally. Add to the list whenever you notice something new or recall something you hadn't previously thought of.

By doing this exercise, you will see your teen in a more positive light, and you will start to focus your attention on the things you love about them, overshadowing the aspects of them you struggle with. It will also make it easier for you to shift your MINDSET during more challenging times.

Conclusion

It's easy to underestimate the impact your perception has on your teen's behaviour and view of themselves. It's also easy to get caught in a critical mindset when your teen constantly challenges you, so I get it. But by making tiny shifts to your mindset, you really can influence your teen's behaviour and strengthen your connection in the process.

Figure 25.

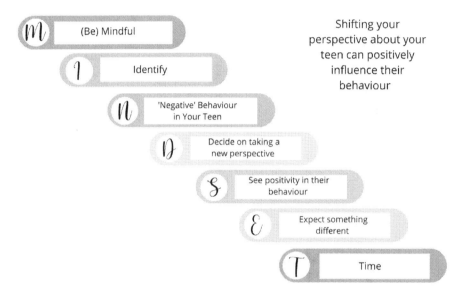

Change Your 'Mindset'

M (Be) Mindful

I Identify

N 'Negative' Behaviour in Your Teen

D Decide on taking a new perspective

S See positivity in their behaviour

E Expect something different

T Time

Shifting your perspective about your teen can positively influence their behaviour

CHAPTER 11

End With the Beginning

(Trigger Warning—Topics of Self-Harm and Attempted Suicide)

Earlier on, I alluded to being a troubled teen and how it influenced both this book and my work with teenagers in general. But perhaps you don't realise just how troubled I was. Do you remember Sadie? I spoke about her struggles with mental health, self-harming, and substance abuse. Well, Sadie was me, and now I want to tell you my story, a story I have rarely shared in as much depth as I will now.

You know a little of my background already, but let me paint a more detailed picture for you. I was literally born and raised in a small village in the English countryside. I remember my family life fondly. We had a big house with land and a pool, and we loved the freedom it afforded my brother and me as kids. My mother stayed at home with us our entire childhoods, doting on us and filling our bellies with delicious food. My father worked hard, leaving the house early so he could be home in time for dinner and our bedtime routine.

My brother is three years older than me, and we had the typical sibling relationship. We both loved and annoyed each other in equal measure. But we were close friends and loyal companions. My brother and I went to local schools and had friends in the village, and it was a time when kids were free to roam. We ran in the fields, climbed trees, and played in the streams, returning home when our tummies rumbled or the sun was setting, whichever came first. It was the quintessential English country upbringing.

But bubbling beneath the surface, there was something I couldn't explain. I was happy at home. I was also sensitive and emotional. I felt everything deeply and was too aware of the darker side of life at far too young an age. I thought seriously about topics I shouldn't have as a girl. I couldn't conceptualise why people hurt others, why there was poverty, animal cruelty, or injustice. I felt guilty and carried responsibility simply because I was a human. I was curious and asked esoteric questions about the meaning of life, and the answers did not satisfy me.

I was also bullied at school for many years. I guess, now looking back, I was an obvious target. I was different and reacted to the bully as she wanted. I was a victim. Due to my sensitive nature, I internalised everything she said, assuming it was true. I started to get weighed down by sadness and self-hatred. The world was a painful place.

I was good at hiding my feelings and kept things largely a secret. My parents knew I was a curious child and quite introverted but were unaware of what was really happening to me. I wrote disturbing poetry, an attempt to purge my darkness, but it didn't work, and I fell further into an abyss. The critical, abusive self-talk got louder and harsher on the inside, and I got more volatile, angry, and withdrawn on the outside.

I think I was about 13 when I first cut myself. I don't recall what triggered it. Or where I even got the idea, to be honest. But I do remember the moment vividly. It was clearly premeditated because I used a kitchen knife, the sharpest I could find. I was so overwhelmed I felt I would burst from the emotions raging inside me. I sat on my bed, legs crossed, and rested my left arm on my knee. Everything stilled as I held the knife to my forearm. My focus intensified, my breathing deepened, and my mind stilled. Even my heartbeat slowed in my chest. I pushed the knife into my skin and slowly dragged it towards me. The pain was sharp, and I gritted my teeth. But the aftermath was worth it. My emotions spilled out with the droplets of blood that formed in the wake of the knife. It was alleviating! Even the aftercare held meaning. I tended to the cut with antiseptic and a bandage, hiding the evidence. The whole experience soothed me. I cut myself with increasing frequency and depth as I no longer felt the same relief the first cut had provided. I see now it worked like any other addiction.

As I got older, I self-harmed in other ways. I found it both placated me and served as a punishment; I had such little self-respect. I started smoking cigarettes at 14, as did my handful of friends. We thought we looked older and "cool." Then came the drinking. It seemed just a natural progression, and in the 90's, it was easy to access pubs and clubs and get served. I was drinking regularly at 15, as so many of us were, especially village kids with nothing else to do. We were stuck in the middle of nowhere, relying on our parents to do anything. The freedom of country life became suffocating.

Marijuana was next on the list. I found it did the most for me. The harsh, self-flagellation quietened when I got stoned, and it brought me to the present moment. I discovered a form of mindfulness. However, it didn't last. The munchies that accompanied smoking weed triggered an eating disorder as a binge starvation cycle started. The dopamine hit from the food washed me with good feelings (something I severely lacked), but the following day, the guilt and shame from gauging was all-encompassing, and I punished myself by restricting what I ate. It became another form of self-harm.

I resembled nothing of the happy and carefree little girl I had been. I was caught in a mess of destructive emotions, and self-hatred was entrenched within me. I felt lost, lonely, and misunderstood. I was scared and saw no way out of the darkness that engulfed me. I thought no one could help me, and the world was not a place I wanted to be. It was then I realised, there was one way out of all the turmoil.

I gathered all the Panadol I could find in the house and added it to my personal stash. Then locked my bedroom door. I felt an eerie calmness and a sense of relief once I had made the decision. I wrote a poem, a suicide note, and placed it by my bed. I took the tablets one at a time with tentative sips of water. There were around 40, as I recall. Then, I climbed into bed and fell asleep with acceptance.

I woke in the night, stomach cramps folding me in two. I only just reached my dustbin before I vomited continuously as my body purged itself of the poison. I finally passed out with exhaustion. No one knew what happened that night for many years to come. I sold my condition as a stomach bug and spent the entire day in bed, sleeping and being nursed by my family. I can't say it was a moment of drastic change. I still drank and smoked cigarettes and weed. I even kept cutting myself, but I knew I wanted to live.

Soon after, my parents found a letter I had written to my best friend, discussing my self-harming. They felt devastated, petrified, and helpless. I felt a flicker of relief. In their desperation, they did everything they thought was right. They spoke to our family GP and sent me to a psychologist. I was angry they did it behind my back, and I didn't engage in therapy. I literally never said a word, and my psychologist actually commended me on it. I felt forced to go and had no connection with the woman. I also didn't know what was going on for me, so how was I meant to talk about it? I didn't make things easy for my parents, and looking back as an adult, I can acknowledge how terrified they must have been.

At 15, I was diagnosed with depression and medicated. It was the start of a long and arduous journey to wellness.

Conclusion

I wanted to share my story to provide insight into how a teenager can spiral out of control and to convey a message that there is hope, no matter how challenging things get with your teen. Both I and many others stand as proof of that. While it's not always easy, it's entirely possible for your teen to not merely survive the adolescent years, as I did, but to thrive during them.

Although I learnt a lot through my degrees, training, and work experience, I believe none were more valuable than my lived experience as a teenager. I managed to lift myself from the lowest place a human can be, a point where I no longer wanted to be alive. I pursued all the strategies I mentioned with Sadie, but for myself. I read extensively, seeking guidance wherever I could find it: in spiritual texts, personal development books, and from self-help gurus. I adopted habits of mindfulness and meditation to remain present and grounded. I taught myself to identify, process, and release my emotions, as well as to communicate my thoughts and feelings. I worked diligently on my self-esteem and self-respect. Persistently, I sought support until I connected with a therapist who helped me untangle the convoluted web that my mind and life had become.

My younger self would not recognise the woman I am today. It is not to say I don't struggle at times; I wouldn't be human if that were the case. But I continue to learn and grow, to treat myself with loving kindness, compassion, and empathy. My daily routine includes meditation and self-care, which are non-negotiable for me and the reason I advocate so strongly for it in others. I embody the strategies in this book as a "recovering troubled teen."

I believe my whole life has brought me to this point. My experiences as a teen, my education, work, and training, as well as my unwavering dedication to personal development and self-care, have all led me to work with parents and their teens. I feel I have come full circle, becoming the person I needed as a teenager. I know I can provide parents with the tools mine needed but did not have access to. I am confident I can help you empower your teen to forge their own way through adolescence, find meaning, discover their purpose, and positively impact the world around them.

I want to clarify: at no point does this book lay blame on anyone or intend to make you feel like a bad parent. I truly believe we all do our best in the moment, with the knowledge and tools we have as the person we are at the time. I hope all the information *Their World* contains helps you better understand your teen. By knowing the strong force adolescence has in driving your teen's behaviour, it gives you the ability to support your teen when they are struggling, guide them through the issues addressed in this book, and help them grow stronger as a result. I'm sure you will have noticed common themes throughout the book and approaches you can apply to almost any situation, ensuring your teen becomes a secure, confident, and productive member of society who thrives as the unique individual they are.

What Next?

If you enjoyed this book, get value from the intriguing information, actionable advice, and secret strategies contained within it, and are eager for more, you can connect with me on any of our socials:

https://www.facebook.com/LauraChappellUniqueParenting

https://www.instagram.com/unique_parenting_2020/

https://twitter.com/UP_TR2020

https://www.linkedin.com/in/laura-chappell-4053a4139/

You can even contact me directly via my email if you have any questions, comments or insights.

Laura@Unique-Parenting.com.au

You can also head over to our website to learn more about my company, Unique Parenting, and my work. A great next step would be to sign up for

our content-rich, no-spam newsletter for weekly-ish advice, useful information, and juicy updates on Parenting Teens successfully through the challenges of adolescence

(the link is on our website and includes a bonus free resource).
https://unique-parenting.com.au

UNIQUE PARENTING

References

Addiction Outreach Clinic. (2023). *8 Personality Traits of Addicts.* Accessed July 12 through

https://addictionoc.com/8-personality-traits-of-addicts/

American Addiction Centers. (2023). *Teenage Addiction Guide for Parents of Addicts: Part 1.* Accessed June 5 2023, through https://americanaddictioncenters.org/rehab-guide/guide-for-parents-i

Anzilotti, A. W. (2022). *Chlamydia.* Accessed June 10 through https://kidshealth.org/en/teens/std-chlamydia.html

Anzilotti, A. W. (2022). *Genital Herpes.* Accessed June 10 through

https://kidshealth.org/en/teens/std-herpes.html

Anzilotti, A. W. (2022). *Gonorrhea.* Accessed June 10 through https://kidshealth.org/en/teens/std-gonorrhea.html

Anzilotti, A. W. (2022). *STDs (Sexually Transmitted Diseases).* Accessed June 10 through https://kidshealth.org/en/teens/std.html

Anzilotti, A. W. (2022). *Trichomoniasis.* Accessed June 10 through https://kidshealth.org/en/teens/std-trichomoniasis.html

American Psychological Society. *Resilience.* Accessed 17 July 2023 through https://www.apa.org/topics/resilience

Arnold, J. Who is Jaylen? Accessed 23 January 2023 through https://www.jaylenschallenge.org/content/who-jaylen

Aronov-Jacoby, S. (2022). *The Benefits of Self-Awareness.* Accessed 7 June 2023 through *https://www.hrh.ca/2022/01/27/the-benefits-of-self-awareness/*

Barlow, D. H., & Durand, V. M. (2012). *Abnormal Psychology. An Integrative Approach.* (6th edition). Wadsworth, Cengage Learning.

Brown, B. (2023). *People with High Emotional Intelligence have these 20 Personality Traits.* Accessed June 2 through https://experteditor.com.au/blog/people-with-high-emotional-intelligence-have-these-personality-traits/

Centre for Addiction and Mental Health. (2023). *Addiction.* Accessed July 12, 2023, through

https://www.camh.ca/en/health-info/mental-illness-and-addiction-index/addiction

Centres for Disease Control and Prevention. (2022). *CDC Fact Sheet: Information for Teens and Young Adults: Staying Healthy and Preventing STDs.* Accessed June 10 through

https://www.cdc.gov/std/life-stages-populations/stdfact-teens.htm

Centres for Disease Control and Prevention. (2022). *Quick Facts on the Risks of E-cigarettes for Kids, Teens and Young Adults.* Accessed June 7 2023, through https://www.cdc.gov/tobacco/basic_information/e-cigarettes/Quick-Facts-on-the-Risks-of-E-cigarettes-for-Kids-Teens-and-Young-Adults.html

Centres for Disease Control and Prevention. (2022). *Teen Drivers and Passengers: Get the Facts.* Accessed June 3 2023, through

https://www.cdc.gov/transportationsafety/teen_drivers/teendrivers_factsheet.html

Cherry, K. (2022). *What is Self-Esteem?* Accessed July 18 2023, through https://www.verywellmind.com/what-is-self-esteem-2795868

Choucair, B. (2023). *E-cigarette Inhalation Device.* Accessed June 7 2023, through https://www.britannica.com/topic/e-cigarette

Clark, C. (2019). *6 Personality Traits Commonly Linked to Addiction.* Accessed July 12 2023, through

https://www.guardianrecoverynetwork.com/drug-and-alcohol-addiction/6-personality-traits-commonly-linked-to-addiction/

Clark University. *Tips For Managing Conflict.* Accessed July16 2023 through https://www.clarke.edu/campus-life/health-wellness/counseling/articles-advice/tips-for-managing-conflict/

Cleveland Clinic. (2022). *Video Game Addiction.* Accessed June 27 2023, through https://my.clevelandclinic.org/health/diseases/23124-video-game-addiction

Common Sense Media. (2021). *The Common Sense Census: Media Use by Tweens and Teens, 2021.*Accessed on June 17 2023, through https://www.commonsensemedia.org/sites/default/files/research/report/8-18-census-integrated-report-final-web_0.pdf

Common Sense Media. (2022). *Teens and Pornography..* Accessed on June 17 2023, through https://www.commonsensemedia.org/sites/default/files/research/report/2022-teens-and-pornography-final-web.pdf

Crisp, R. J., & Turner, R. N. (2010). (2nd edition). *Essential Social Psychology.* Sage.

Destinations. (2022). *Why are Teens More Susceptible to Drug Addiction?* Accessed June 4 2023, through https://www.destinationsforteens.com/destinations-blog/why-teens-are-more-susceptible-to-drug-addiction/

Devito, J. A. (2009). *The Interpersonal Communication Book.* (12th edition). Pearson Education, Inc.

Doppel. (2020). *Exploring the 'Fight-or-Flight' Response.* Accessed July 17 2023, through

https://feeldoppel.com/blogs/news/exploring-the-fight-or-flight-response

Eating Disorder Hope. (2017). *Food Addiction: Causes, Symptoms, Signs & Treatment Help.* Accessed July 2 2023, through https://www.eatingdisorderhope.com/information/food-addiction

Ekman, P. (2007). *Emotions Revealed.* (2nd edition). Holts Paperback

Emmanuel, M. & Bokor, B. R. (2022). *Tanner Stages.* Accessed July 20 2023 through https://www.ncbi.nlm.nih.gov/books/NBK470280/

E-Safety Commissioner. (2021). *The Digital Lives of Aussie Teens.* Accessed June 2 2023, through *https://www.esafety.gov.au/sites/default/files/2021-02/The%20digital%20lives%20of%20Aussie%20teens.pdf*

EU Business School. (2021). *9 Characteristics of Emotionally Intelligent People*. Accessed June 2 2023, through https://www.euruni.edu/blog/9-characteristics-of-emotionally-intelligent-people/

Evans, O. G. (2023). *Maslow's Hierarchy of Needs*. Accessed 19 July 2023 through https://www.simplypsychology.org/maslow.html

Fadhilah, W. (2012). *Effects and Consequences of Teenage Pregnancy*. Accessed June 2 2023, through http://www.myhealth.gov.my/en/effects-a-consequences-ofteenage-pregnancy/

Gitnux. (2023). *The Most Surprising Teen Statistics and Trends in 2023*. Accessed June 7 2023, through *https://blog.gitnux.com/teens-statistics/*

Goldberg, R. (2023). *Screen Time and Step Counts Determine Overweight and Obesity Risk*. Accessed July 13 2023, through https://www.psychiatryadvisor.com/home/topics/child-adolescent-psychiatry/lower-step-count-and-higher-screen-time-lead-to-increased-overweight-and-obesity-risk/

Goleman, D. & Boyatzis, R. (2017). *Emotional Intelligence has 12 Elements. Which Do You Need to Work On?* Accessed July 23 2023, through https://hbr.org/2017/02/emotional-intelligence-has-12-elements-which-do-you-need-to-work-on

Growing Up in Australia. The Longitudinal Study of Australian Children. (2021). *Alcohol Use Among Teens Allowed to Drink at Home. Growing Up in Australia Snapshot Series – Issue 2*. Accessed July 1 2023 https://growingupinaustralia.gov.au/sites/default/files/publication-documents/lsac-snapshot-2-drinking-at-home.pdf

Hammerslag, L. R. & Gulley, J. M. (2015). *Sex Differences in Behaviour and Neural Development and their Role in Adolescent Vulnerability to Substance*

Use. Accessed June 12 2023
https://www.ncbi.nlm.nih.gov/pmc/articles/PMC4603997/

Health Direct. (2021). *Stress.* Accessed 25 June 2023, through
https://www.healthdirect.gov.au/stress

Hinders, D. (2017). *6 Personality Traits Linked to Addiction.* Accessed July
12 2023, through https://stjosephinstitute.com/6-personality-traits-linked-
to-addiction/

Hull, M. (2023). *Drugs Commonly Used by Teens.* Accessed June 12 2023,
through https://www.therecoveryvillage.com/teen-
addiction/drug/commonly-abused-drugs/

Jensen, F. E., & Ellis Nutt, A. (2015). *The Teenage Brain. A Neuroscientist's
Survival Guide to Raising Adolescents and Young Adults.* Harper

Kids Encyclopedia Facts. (2023). *Jazz Jennings Facts for Kids.* Accessed
January 14 2023, through https://kids.kiddle.co/Jazz_Jennings

LoveOurGirls. Miley Dias. Accessed January 14 2023, through
https://logpledge.org/miley-dias/

Lucker, E. (2022). *Are Video Games, Screens Another Addiction?* Accessed
June 27 2023, through https://www.mayoclinichealthsystem.org/hometown-
health/speaking-of-health/are-video-games-and-screens-another-addiction

Martin, A. (2023). *Navigating Puberty: The Tanner Stages.* Accessed July 20
2023, through

https://www.healthline.com/health/parenting/stages-of-puberty

Mayo Clinic. (2022). *Sexually Transmitted Disease (STD) Symptoms.*
Accessed June 10 through https://www.mayoclinic.org/diseases-

conditions/sexually-transmitted-diseases-stds/in-depth/std-symptoms/art-20047081

Mayo Clinic. (2022). *Teen Suicide: What parents need to Know.* Accessed June 22 through

https://www.mayoclinic.org/healthy-lifestyle/tween-and-teen-health/in-depth/teen-suicide/art-20044308

Mayo Clinic. (2023). *Stress Symptoms: Effects on Your Body and Behavior.* Accessed June 26 through https://www.mayoclinic.org/healthy-lifestyle/stress-management/in-depth/stress-symptoms/art-20050987

Miller, R.S (2012). *Intimate Relationships.* (6th edition). McGraw-Hill.

Nationwide Children's. (2016). *Risks of Teen Pregnancy.* Accessed June 2 2023, through https://www.nationwidechildrens.org/family-resources%20education/700childrens/2016/10/risks-of-teen-pregnancy

Newport Academy. (2023). *Identifying Different Types of Self-harm in Teens.* Accessed June 18 2023, through https://www.newportacademy.com/resources/mental-health/self-injury/

NSW Kids and Families. (2014). *Youth Health Resource Kit: An Essential Guide for Workers.* Accessed June 5 2023, through

https://www.health.nsw.gov.au/kidsfamilies/youth/Publications/youth-health-resource-kit.pdf

Partnership to End Addiction. (2023). *Signs of Drug Use in Teens.* Accessed June 6 2023, through https://drugfree.org/article/signs-of-drug-use-in-teens/

Peterson, C. C. (2010). *Looking Forward Through the Lifespan. Developmental Psychology.* (5th edition). Pearson.

Robinson, L., Segal, J., & Smith, M. (2023). *Effective Communication.* Accessed July 7 2023, through https://www.helpguide.org/articles/relationships-communication/effective-communication.htm

Rolston, A. & Lloyd-Richardson, E. *What is Emotional Regulation and How Do We Do It?* Accessed July 16 2023, through https://selfinjury.bctr.cornell.edu/perch/resources/what-is-emotion-regulationsinfo-brief.pdf

Rosenberg, M. (2015). *Nonviolent Communication: A Language of Life: Life-Changing Tools for Healthy Relationships.* (3rd edition). Puddledancer Press.

Salerno, J. (2023). *What is an At-Risk Youth - Part 1.* Accessed June 3 2023, through https://possibilitiesforchange.org/what-is-an-at-risk-youth-part-1/

Salerno, J. (2023). *What is an At-Risk Youth - Part 2.* Accessed June 3 2023, through https://possibilitiesforchange.org/what-is-an-at-risk-youth-part-2/

Sanci, L., Webb, M. & Hocking, J. S. (2018). *Risk-taking Behaviour in Adolescents.* Accessed July 12 2023, through https://www1.racgp.org.au/ajgp/2018/december/risk-taking-behaviour-in-adolescents

Segal, J., Smith. M., Robinson, L. & Shubin, J. (2023). *Improving Emotional Intelligence (EQ).* Accessed June 1 2023, through https://www.helpguide.org/articles/mental-health/emotional-intelligence-eq.htm

Segal, J., Smith. M., Robinson, L. & Smith, M. (2023). *What is Conflict?* Accessed July 20 2023, through https://www.helpguide.org/articles/relationships-communication/conflict-resolution-skills.htm

Shultz, D. P., & Shultz, S. E. (2013). *Theories of Personality*. (10th edition). Wadsworth, Cengage Learning.

Shultz, M. C. & Trevino, T. A. (2021). Genital Warts (HPV). Accessed June 10 through https://kidshealth.org/en/teens/std-warts.html

Slager, E. *9 Warning Signs of Exercise Addiction*. Accessed July 6 2023, through https://www.waldeneatingdisorders.com/blog/9-warning-signs-of-exercise-addiction/

Smart, C. *What if My Teen is The Bully?* Accessed June 7 2023, through *https://www.raisingteenagers.com.au/what-if-my-teen-is-the-bully/*

Stoewen, D. L. (2017). *Dimensions of Wellness: Change your Habits, Change your Life*. Accessed July 26 2023, through https://www.ncbi.nlm.nih.gov/pmc/articles/PMC5508938/

Taylor, M. (2022). *What Does Fight, Flight, Freeze, Fawn Mean?* Accessed July 17 2023, through https://www.webmd.com/mental-health/what-does-fight-flight-freeze-fawn-mean

The University of Queensland. (2021). *Excess screen time impacting teen mental health*. Accessed July 17 2023, through https://www.uq.edu.au/news/article/2021/08/excess-screen-time-impacting-teen-mental-health

TheraPlatform. (2023). *What is Emotional Literacy?* Accessed July21 2023 through https://www.theraplatform.com/blog/486/what-is-emotional-literacy

Thompson, D. (2023). *Too Much Screen Time May Raise Risk of Mental Health Disorders Among Kids*. Accessed June 25 2023, through https://www.upi.com/Health_News/2023/03/29/screen-time-kids-mental-health/4781680111073/

UNESCO. (2018). *New Data Reveal that 1 in 3 Teens is Bullied Worldwide.* Accessed June 7 2023, through https://www.unesco.org/en/articles/new-data-reveal-one-out-three-teens-bullied-worldwide?TSPD_101_R0=080713870fab2000d0a46f42ffa8f030e9a84898157 bf96add3ff58cc03d5b4c7770013d5dc3dafe08ead86015143000f1561651ee96c 9bb7cc88a59c513432b27e77a8bb4ba982643e75b38c725df5e0dc409dae86804 3fff537ffae34a67f6

University of Ottawa. (2019). *Impulsive Behaviour Linked to Sleep and Screen Time.* Accessed June 24 2023, through https://www.sciencedaily.com/releases/2019/08/190814113931.htm

Vaghefi, S. (2023). *Culture Vs Society : Similarities, Differences, Examples.* Accessed July 8 2023, through https://helpfulprofessor.com/culture-vs-society/#google_vignette

Vojinovic, I. (2023). *Heart-breaking Cyberbullying Statistics for 2023.* Accessed July 15 2023, through *https://dataprot.net/statistics/cyberbullying-statistics/*

Wake Forest University. *The Difference Between Feelings and Emotions.* Accessed Jun 28 through https://counseling.online.wfu.edu/blog/difference-feelings-emotions/

Weber State University. *Self-esteem.* Accessed July 18 through https://www.weber.edu/CounselingCenter/self-esteem.html

Weir, K. (2016). *The Risks of Earlier Puberty.* Accessed June 7 2023, through https://www.apa.org/monitor/2016/03/puberty

Weiten, W. (2010). *Psychology Themes & Variations.* (8th edition). Wadsworth, Cengage Learning.

Wells, D. (2023). *12 Dangerous TikTok Challenges Trending.* Accessed June 16 2023, through https://www.myhighplains.com/life-health/12-dangerous-tiktok-challenges-trending/

World Health Organisation. (2021). *Mental Health of Adolescents.* Accessed 22 June 2023, through https://www.who.int/news-room/fact-sheets/detail/adolescent-mental-health#:~:text=It%20is%20estimated%20that%203.6,and%20unexpected%20changes%20in%20mood.

World Population Review. (2023). *Age of Consent by Country 2023.* Accessed July 14 2023, through https://worldpopulationreview.com/country-rankings/age-of-consent-by-country

World Population Review. (2023). *Drinking Age by Country 2023.* Accessed July 6 2023, through https://worldpopulationreview.com/country-rankings/drinking-age-by-country

Wood White, K. (2018). *Syphilis.* Accessed June 10 through https://kidshealth.org/en/teens/std-syphilis.html

THANK YOU FOR READING MY BOOK!

DOWNLOAD YOUR FREE GIFTS

Just to say thank you for buying and reading my book, I would love to give you a Free Resources Bundle, no strings attached!

To Download Now, Visit:

I appreciate your interest in my book, and value your feedback as it helps me improve future versions of this book. I would appreciate it if you could leave your invaluable review on Amazon.com with your feedback. Thank you!

Printed in Great Britain
by Amazon

30842133R00148